D0849210

SPECK

THE LIFE AND TIMES OF SPENCER PENROSE

BY ROBERT C. OLSON

WESTERN REFLECTIONS PUBLISHING COMPANY®

Lake City, CO

© 2008 Robert C. Olson
All rights reserved. No part of this book may be reproduced
in any form without permission in writing from the author.

ISBN 978-1-932738-50-6

Library of Congress Control Number: 2008921759

Cover and book design: Laurie Goralka Design
Cover painting: Julian Story

First Edition

Printed in Canada

Western Reflections Publishing Company®
P.O. Box 1149, 951 N. Highway 149
Lake City, CO 81235
1-800-993-4490
westref@montrose.net
www.westernreflectionspub.com

PREFACE

In charting the life of Spencer Penrose, there were certain times and events not fully documented. These blind areas have been filled in with what information could be culled from the corresponding records of the specific time and the memories of key individuals. Since Penrose has become such a legend, it is sometimes difficult to separate fact from fiction.

DEDICATION

This book is dedicated to my father Raymond L. Olson. He was the son of a large Mormon family whose forbears came across the plains with Brigham Young. They settled in Logan, Utah, where Ray graduated from Utah State University and later wound up on the editorial staff of the *Salt Lake Tribune*.

As a champion of the Repeal of Prohibition, he served as president of the Utah Constitutional Convention that, on December 5, 1933, made Utah the 36th and final state necessary to ratify the 21st Amendment which abolished national Prohibition.

During the late 1930s he worked in the nation's capital with the Roosevelt Administration's Office of Information. He spent most of his later life writing because, as he often said, "I have printer's ink in my blood."

He was a thoughtful, kind and generous person, interested in others, and often provided advice and guidance when appropriate. After a distinguished career in communications, he passed away in the early 1980s, leaving his adopted son and family and a large array of devoted friends.

ACKNOWLEDGEMENTS

A number of individuals have helped me with this book and gave me a great deal of confidence and enthusiasm. Terry Britt, a mining petroleum geologist and long-time friend, emphasized the stature of the Geological Society of America (GSA) and emphasized the importance of Dick Penrose and Daniel Jackling. Arthur Church, an old school chum from Kansas City and now a resident of Colorado Springs, assisted immensely with my research pertaining to the El Pomar Foundation and the El Paso Club, including a tour of the appropriate historic Penrose landmarks in the Springs.

Sandra Dallas, a well known author and friend, strongly reminded me that you don't have to be a Hemingway to write a book successfully. I received enormous encouragement and prodding from Mary Ann Lee, a real estate executive and friend, to get the book published. Kam Martin, a former professional editor with experience in New York, helped me with her precise and skillful editing Sara Sheldon, former employee of Darcy Communications and now a well-established writer, clarified the operations and functions in today's publishing world.

Of course, my "other half", Sandy Olson, lovingly provided objectivity and suggestions on my literary attempts. The publishing staff of Western Reflections also made it easier, and actually exciting, satisfying and fulfilling to publish this book.

Thank you all!

Robert C. Olson

TABLE OF CONTENTS

FOREWORD

In the annals of American history there was probably no greater two-fisted, hard-drinking, high-rolling tycoon of the Rockies than Spencer, or "Speck," Penrose. He was an unforgettable multi-millionaire who found his fortune in the turmoil of the rip-roaring, gold mining boom days and lived to enjoy it to the fullest possible extent.

Everyone knew the soft-spoken Philadelphia blue blood with a Harvard accent who made things happen. Wearing a wide-brimmed hat, English riding boots, and a neatly trimmed mustache became his trademark. He had the gut determination of a prospector, the readiness to put up his fists and fight at the untimely raise of an eyebrow, and an almost artist-like sensitivity to prepare himself for any situation.

His extraordinary seventy-four years were diverse, fast-moving, and explosive. He was loved, feared, hated, and cherished by those caught in the wake of his dynamic life. He became realtor, gold baron, copper king, manufacturer, resort operator, community builder, world traveler, public benefactor, philanthropist, president maker, and arch enemy of prohibition.

He came to Colorado where he started making his millions at a time when he did not have to divvy up money to the government for income taxes. He was a world-renowned magnate, speculator, showman, cynic, dreamer, sentimentalist, hard-boiled businessman, and citizen of the world. But always, he reigned supreme in his realm of the Rocky Mountains. He played hard and worked hard to satisfy a lust for accomplishments of any kind, as long as they were on a grand scale...the celebrated Broadmoor Hotel splashed in splendor...his fabulous wine cellar...his political bets of $50,000, $100,000, $175,000, when most any multi-millionaire would have been considered reckless to have wagered $25,000 or even $10,000.

The story of his life has conflict between Speck and his father whom he loved and respected and who, alone, raised him and his five brothers. It has romance, the love between two aristocrats who married late in life to find a lasting relationship. It is filled with action, the kind you don't hear about anymore, of a rich boy who took boxing lessons at Harvard and quickly found practical use for his well-developed skill. It shows the depth of a man's full life, lived to the hilt from the top social set in Philadelphia to the rough and tumble mountain gold camps of Colorado, to the cosmopolitan circles of world travelers. It has sex, found in the burly mining camp bordellos and the tinseled glitter of prostitute-filled saloons where fighters trained in the rear. And finally, it has entertainment, captured in the bustling story of a man and his insatiable desire to do more — drink when it is outlawed, turn tides of political philosophies, and speak out against people and issues where angels fear to tread.

Penrose was a rich and shiftless ne'er-do-well with a free spirit who finally planted his feet in the Colorado

Rockies and became a giant — certainly the most successful and exciting man in the short-lived gold mining boom
period. He became a person who was singularly responsible for literally moving mountains — the gigantic Bingham
open pit mine that is now a principal source of the world's
largest copper mining company, Kennecott. And he became
the inn keeper of the world at the fabulous Broadmoor
Hotel that he built, where kings and presidents met,
and where not even Prohibition could hold back the flow
of champagne.

The story of Spencer Penrose's life includes many incredible and colorful characters whose lives are interwoven with
his. His brother Dick, who was and is still considered one of
the country's greatest geologists, was on a first name basis
with President Herbert Hoover, who openly and intensely
respected him as a man and as a professional. His beautiful mother was the toast of Philadelphia's elite. His father,
Dr. Penrose, wanted his boys to know not only the academic
part of education but the seamy side of life, too. The per-
sonable Julie captured the confirmed bachelor after Speck
passed age forty, when normally the dye is cast for bach-
elorhood. Another brother, the huge, robust, and powerful
Senator Boies Penrose, was a strong man and "kingmaker" of
the Republican party who tapped Warren Harding as presidential nominee. Many other characters influenced the life of
Speck, each contributing a step on the road of a rich man's
unsung son to the stature of a king.

Decades after his death, the image of Spencer Penrose
still lives in Colorado where his everlasting impression was
made. Although Penrose played a paramount part in the
history of the West, the colorful saga of his incredible life
has never been told in its entirety. On the following pages,

stretching out almost three-quarters of a century, from the year the Civil War ended to two-years-to-the-day before Pearl Harbor, unfolds the story that has become a legend... the life of Spencer Penrose.

CHAPTER I
AT THE FOOT
OF PIKES PEAK

For a Harvard graduate who could down a pitcher of beer in thirty-seven seconds and survive water-front brawls in dives along Philadelphia's Schuylkill River, the rugged and rollicking atmosphere of Cripple Creek, Colorado, at the peak of its gold boom in 1893, was just the ticket. Twenty-eight year old Spencer Penrose, better known as "Speck" and an offspring of a blue blood Philadelphia family, had become the best hustler of mountain real estate in town and led the liveliest group, the "Socialites," who set the pace for drinking, partying, and fighting. Already billed as "The Largest Gold Camp on Earth," Cripple Creek was the playground for these Ivy League, derby-donned dandies, most of whom were grubstaked by their affluent families either to satisfy their own lust for adventure or simply so their parents could get ride of them.

After Speck jockeyed his way into managing property in Cripple Creek, he hired one of his Harvard classmates to help solve his biggest problem, rent collection. One morning at 7:30, Speck joined his new man to show him the ropes. One of his clients owned the parlor house rented to a Denver madam whose professional name was Lola Livingstone.

The first stop was at Lola's place where Speck's collector was to collect forty-five dollars. Speck waited outside in the buckboard. He waited and waited; went to the Topic Hall for a cup of coffee and came out just as his Harvard protégé emerged from the parlor house. When Speck asked what took so long and if he got his money, the tenderfoot collector said that he had had a long talk with the proprietress, and they decided that he ought to take it out in trade. The new man was not fired immediately. He had to work long enough to pay back the forty-five dollars to Speck.

In the early 1890s, the mountain town's sin street, Myers Avenue, became world renowned for its gaudy display of corruption. Standard newspaper copy, describing an event at the Dawson Club, in the *Cripple Creek Times* set the tone for the times, "One of the witnesses said that as the man lay dying some of the crowd urged him to the bar for one last drink."

In 1915 after Speck's gold mill trust was formed, he became owner of several mines including the Portland. Two muckers at the mine, Bernie and William Harrison, from Manassa, Utah, were also professional boxers. Speck and his friends promoted a fight in Cripple Creek by matching one of the Harrison brothers with George Coplen, the town giant. After training in the backrooms of local bars, the fighters were deemed ready and the match was finally set in the Butte Opera House for one of the largest crowds ever assembled in the gold camp. At the eleventh hour, the older brother, after taking one good look at the huge opponent, touted his younger brother to take his place. Since both fought under the same name, few fans knew the difference. This fight, staged by Speck and his side-kicks, became the first major professional fight for young William Harrison, or as the brothers called themselves, "Jack Dempsey."

Speck had many bouts himself with politicians, prohibitionists, and even Wall Street capitalists. He was extremely finicky. Speck disliked those who whispered in his presence, detested dial phones, but most of all he distrusted New York capitalists. This was not only because they ruined his friend Charlie MacNeill, but because they trimmed David Moffat, who had made a fortune in Cripple Creek and lost it in an attempt to build a railroad over the Rockies, counting on a verbal pledge of assistance from Wall Street financiers. Speck had warned MacNeill against the New York crowd. "Stick with the Guggenheims. They're not only smart but they're honest, which is more than you can say about the Wall Street highbinders."

Besides Speck's brother Dick, the eminent geologist who had helped him immensely with his mining projects, one of the most influential people in his earlier life was his oldest brother Boies, the powerful U.S. Senator from Pennsylvania. While Boies was grooming Ohio Senator Warren Harding for the presidential nomination in 1920, reports reached him of an unfavorable speech made by his candidate. As a result, he ordered Harding to make no more public addresses until the time he was elected president. Right or wrong, Boies' strategy worked. Many other well-known politicians were close to the Penroses. Among them were Herbert Hoover, a friend of Dick's from his earlier engineering days, and the son of America's least-known president, Chester Arthur, who was one of Speck's best friends.

Prior to the beginning of Prohibition, it was rumored that Speck had bought a trainload of bonded liquor to last him through the drought. The rumor indicated that he stored his immense stock in one of his Cripple Creek mines. Immediately there was a rush of liquor prospectors that threatened to eclipse the gold stampede of the 1890s. They became so troublesome that guards had to be placed at the Penrose mining properties, appearing to confirm the suspicions. Groups of Colorado's most distinguished bootleggers formed a syndicate to hijack the "million dollar lode" by buying the adjoining worked-out mine owned by Penrose and digging through into the hiding place. Speck played coy. He told them that he wished to retain the property for "old times sake," but of course, "if the price was right...!" Finally the syndicate bought the mine and put their plan into operation — finding nothing. The liquor had been stored in a bonded warehouse. The befuddled bootleggers were left holding an empty hole in the ground. According to one, it was the first time in history a mine had been "salted" with a million dollars worth of whiskey.

Celebrities, like politicians and movie stars, often stayed at Speck's Broadmoor Hotel located just over Pikes Peak from Cripple Creek in Colorado Springs. One of them was humorist Will Rogers, for whom Speck built the "Shrine of the Sun" above his Broadmoor Hotel on Cheyenne Mountain, south of the city. Although Rogers' most quoted remark "I never met a man I didn't like" most likely applied to his Colorado friend, Speck, one wonders if he could have actually penetrated the famous Speck Penrose poker face. It is doubtful because as an article in the Colorado press stated, "No one ever got behind the dead-pan expression with the sardonic cocked eyebrow to discover the real Penrose." If the entire story of his life were told, however, maybe the true Spencer Penrose would be revealed.

CHAPTER II
REDDEST OF
BLUE BLOODS

It all began at 1331 Spruce Street in Philadelphia the year the Civil War ended. Spencer Penrose was born at that impeccable address on November 2, 1865. His father, Dr. Richard Alexander Fullerton Penrose, was an obstetrician. His mother, Sarah Hannah Boies Penrose, had already given birth to four boys, the first having died at birth. So Speck started off with three older brothers.

After being brought into the world, Speck was placed in a hand carved wooden crib that had a headboard inscribed with the family motto, "Ubique Fidelis." Each one of his brothers, Boies, 5, Charles Bingham, 3, and Richard Alexander Fullerton Jr., 2, had used the same family heirloom.

The Penrose residence on Spruce Street was a three-story structure built of brick and brownstone, featuring long narrow windows and a massive front door with a brass knocker. It stood in the center of what historians considered the heart of the patriotic universe, only a few blocks from Independence Hall, Betsy Ross's home and Ben Franklin's grave. Philadelphians referred to it as the Eighth Ward, an important and affluent political section of the city. It was the home of the aristocratic blue bloods who were considered starchy enough to bring stiffness to the whole nation. Both Dr. Penrose and his wife were proud of their heritage so they made certain that their children were aware of it. The Penrose boys were sixth generation Americans from a family who traced its ancestry back to England and Roger Bigod, Earl of Norfolk, in the 17th century. Dr. Penrose descended directly from William Biddle, proprietor of the province of New Jersey. His great-grandfather Clement Biddle Penrose was Thomas Jefferson's commissioner of the Louisiana Territory, and his father Charles Bingham was treasury solicitor under President William Harrison. His mother was Valeria Fullerton Biddle. The first American Penrose was Bartholomew, an Englishman who gave up his ship-building business in Bristol only to resume it again in Philadelphia in partnership with William Penn in 1700. Wildest of their forebears was Mad Anthony Wayne, an Indian fighter who married their great, great, great aunt.

Mrs. Penrose could claim relationship — and frequently did — to the household of Lord Baltimore, founder of Maryland. It was pure colonial stock, both English Quaker and Roman Catholic. She descended from William Hubbard, one of the earliest graduates of Harvard College in 1642. Her father was Jeremiah Smith Boies, prominent and wealthy merchant of Boston, whose father had helped erect the barricades for the defense of Bunker Hill during the Revolution.

There was a long line of intermarriages between the Penroses and such financially powerful Philadelphia names as the Wardells, the Drexels, the Spencers, the Binghams, and others. Dr. Penrose reflected that it was a heritage that the boys could call upon with great satisfaction.

The doctor was a fit man with a trim figure. When he stood perfectly erect, which he generally did, he was just under six feet tall. His most noticeable feature was a large, long nose that descended into the middle of his walrus mustache. His light sandy hair with long sideburns receded far back on his wrinkled forehead. He was a dowdy dresser who unconsciously conformed to the conservative style.

With the Civil War over, the doctor was no longer vitally needed at Satterlee U.S.A. General Hospital, one of the largest Union Army hospitals, located in Philadelphia. Dr. Penrose, M.D., L.L.D. had tended to the wounded from the battle fronts during the epic four-year struggle. However, he was anxious to fully resume his professional life. A well-qualified intellectual, he had won wide distinction and some wealth in Philadelphia as an obstetrician and medical professor. He started to devote more time, energy, and pecuniary resources to his medical practice, his investments, and his professorship at the University of Pennsylvania Medical School where he specialized in obstetrics and diseases peculiar to women and children. This was a specialty he fell into quite naturally since he liked being involved in the creation of new life. It gave him a feeling of great satisfaction and some manipulative power. He also considered women and children the most vulnerable, and often helpless, targets of disease. Outwardly, he appeared very clinical, but inwardly he thought of medicine with more of a personal involvement and dedication than most doctors. He had graduated from Dickinson College in Carlisle, Pennsylvania, and received his medical degree at the University of Pennsylvania in 1849. Dr. Penrose, who was immensely proud of his rank as a member of the College of Physicians, had helped to establish the University of Pennsylvania, and Children's Hospitals in Philadelphia.

While his formal and meticulous bedside manner created a stilted image, his patients, colleagues, and students respected him. The young men he taught also admired him, not only because of his skill as a professor but due to his lofty, well-deserved and permanently-established station in the medical field. Once, when rumor had it that Dr. Penrose planned to resign from the faculty, the students circulated a petition urging him to stay on. He was flattered but kept his feelings well concealed.

Although the war had been over for seven months, Dr. Penrose still devoted some of his time to wounded Civil War veterans at Satterlee — a fact that Mrs. Penrose often proudly pointed out to her boys. Of course, the doctor had to admit that he played a small part in the Civil War compared to their second cousin, General William Henry Penrose, whose war laurels fit handsomely alongside other American patriots in the family. General Penrose had led the Union army around the western frontier, nursed Kit Carson back to health after a critical illness, founded Ft. Lyons in southern Colorado, and had an assistant nurse who was known as Buffalo Bill Cody.

As Dr. Penrose busied himself with his profession, his wife Hannah gradually recovered from the birth of her fourth child. She was a handsome, articulate woman who possessed an air of loftiness. She had an attractive figure that complimented her clothes, and her gorgeous blue eyes emphasized her classic profile. She was exceedingly conscious of dominating any situation and did so painlessly. Her looks readily attracted attention and her intelligence made conversation easy. Mrs. Penrose was perpetually involved with the Daughters of the American Revolution, rolling bandages at the hospital, sipping tea, or filling in for her sewing circle. Through it

Speck's father and mother, Dr. Richard Alexander Fullerton Penrose and Sarah Hannah Boies Penrose, resided at 1331 Spruce Street in Philadelphia. At the time it was in the affluent center of the city. Here, this socially prominent couple raised six energetic sons.
R.L. Olson Personal Collection

all she occupied herself in the cold, formal ritual of maintaining the family prestige among the elite.

Life in the Penrose household was much like life in any one of the stately mansions along Spruce Street — cultured and cold. However, the Penroses were a well-matched couple. Hannah's conscientious socializing complemented the doctor's extreme standoffishness, which was emphasized by a preoccupation with his profession. Though she tried to be a considerate mother, her live-in help made it possible for her to devote the majority of her time to social and community affairs. The result was an avid socialite mother, so busy on away-from-home functions that little time was left for her children, and a rigid, disciplinarian father who had no time for boyish pranks or any other frivolities. The prospects of a warm family life for the new Penrose baby seemed remote. That is not to say that no love existed in the Penrose family, but there was a lack of open affection.

The pattern for bringing up children in this environment consisted of learning from tutors and private schools, with affection often provided by governesses, nurses, maids, cooks, and servants. There was a cook to prepare their meals and give them snacks, maids to groom their rooms, and stable attendants to take them for rides around the town.

With the help of their staff of domestics, the Penroses were able to entertain easily and often. Now, with the war over, there would be more time and opportunity for parties, so Hannah Penrose made appropriate preparations in her household. In Philadelphia society, Dr. and Mrs. Penrose were popular hosts, known for their tasteful dinners and impressive list of guests, which they enthusiastically enjoyed. At these events, lively dinner conversations ranged from politics to the problems of finding good domestic help. During this entertainment the children were kept completely occupied in their own private sanctuary.

The big house on Spruce Street was filled with delicately-carved woodwork and it featured a living room fireplace that was taller than five-year-old Boies. The dining room, often the scene of society dinners where as many as two dozen could be seated stiffly, sat stage-like a few steps higher than the living room. Oil portraits of notable relatives like Mad Anthony Wayne, Bartholomew Penrose, and Jeremiah Boies were scattered throughout the house. The Penrose servants lived in separate quarters behind the house and their stables could be seen from the back window of the big house, half a block away on Juniper Street.

When the time came for a surname that would be suitable for the fourth boy, the Penroses searched the family tree, just as they had done for their other children. The doctor's great, great grandfather, Reverend Elihu Spencer, had been among the first graduates of Yale University in the class of 1746, distinguished himself in the ministry, and served as a trustee at Princeton. So "Spencer" became the name for the youngest Penrose.

Soon Spencer gave way to "Speck," as the feisty little boy joined his brothers, Boies, Tal (Charles), and Dick, in the scheme of growing up among Philadelphia's rich upper class. By the time Speck had climbed to his feet, his mother gave birth to still another boy on August 2, 1867. Again the parents selected a name that they discovered in their family archives. Francis Boies Penrose was christened in the same manner as his brothers — at the foot of the pulpit in Phila-delphia's principal Episcopal Church. Because the Penroses soon recognized certain traits about the infant they decided on an appropriate nickname. So, like Tal and Speck, he was tagged "Friday."

To Hannah Penrose, having babies became a way of life. Counting her first son who died, she had now given birth to six boys. Her child-bearing came to an end though on March 10, 1869, with the birth of her seventh, Phillip Thomas Penrose. Like Friday, Phillip was observed only with remote curiosity by the four older boys — Boies, Tal, Dick and Speck. The two youngest Penroses became a team, just as Boies and Tal appeared to be an inseparable pair. This left five-year-old Dick and three-year-old Speck, the loners, who went their own independent ways.

By the time Phillip took his first step, Boies, Tal and Dick began to show signs of becoming good students. Speck's progress was still questionable and Friday was too young to be judged. Dr. Penrose observed closely the scholastic habits of the four oldest boys. Although Boies possessed a keen mind with an inordinate capacity to absorb what he read and heard, he was lazy and arrogant even before he reached his teens. Both Tal and Dick pursued their studies earnestly. Speck was the plodder, anxious to keep up with his older brothers but unable to match their talents for learning.

Just across the street from the Penrose house, three spinsters ran a private school — Misses Houghs — that included kindergarten and the first two grades. This was the first school the Penrose boys attended. Later they entered Dr. Chase's Boys School over Mr. Gray's grocery store at 16th and Spruce Streets. Dr. Chase was a Harvard graduate and a learned man, but he had a difficult time controlling a boisterous collection of youngsters. In addition to Dr. Chase's, the boys had tutors for their entrance into college preparatory school.

Since the Penroses were members of Philadelphia's largest Episcopal Church, it was natural to enroll the boys in the Protestant Episcopal Academy, considered one of the best prep schools in the city. This posh, and quite private, school provided a curriculum designed to prepare students for the Ivy League school of their family's choice.

The Penrose boys were by no means sissies, but their parents went to great lengths to shelter them from those ruffians outside the social strata in which they lived. Fortunately, other children in the same situation provided them with playmates and friends. The Penrose brothers had their squabbles like any other red-blooded American boys. If any one series of events highlighted their formative years, it was Hannah Penrose's shock at discovering that her boys actually organized gang fights with students from other private schools.

When fist fights or wrestling between the boys occurred, a horrified Hannah Penrose quickly separated them and gave stiff reprimands for their misbehavior. But it was a different case when Dr. Penrose caught them fighting. Rather than breaking it up, he studied the situation to see if there were any signs of unusual strength, coordination, or potential skill. So the boys did not know what to expect from their father. Sometimes he would watch them fight; other times he would scold them severely. Normally a firm disciplinarian, Dr. Penrose enjoyed his quirk. This activity provided one of the only positive thoughts he consistently had about Speck since the boy possessed a particularly violent swing with his fists.

In his memoirs, Dick Penrose gave his reaction to some of the neighborhood brawls.

> Episcopal Academy was presided over by Dr. Edward Robins, one of the kindest, most sympathetic men I have ever met. Though I greatly respected Dr. Robins, my main recollection of the Episcopal Academy was when we boys used to start in a body around the back streets between

Juniper and 13th streets to make raids on the boys at Dr. Fairie's School. They were real events to us and more important with their bruises and blows than the serious studies and prayers at the Episcopal Academy.

The Penrose boys respected their parents' prohibition against associating with boys of lesser social rank. The three older ones did not cultivate any close relationships, consequently they had no special friends. On the other hand, Speck did find a congenial and acceptable pal. One of Dr. Penrose's associates in the medical profession, Dr. Charles Pendleton Tutt, had moved to Philadelphia from Florida to study at the University of Pennsylvania, graduating with high honors in 1856. He had an only son, Charles Leaming, just one year older than Speck. Although young Tutt's ancestors did not come over on the Mayflower, he was considered socially acceptable as a playmate for the well-born Speck, chiefly because of their fathers' association.

In 1875, by the time Boies reached fifteen, he had become a lumbering, awkward boy. While the next three Penrose brothers were physically strong, the two youngest boys did not attain a similar stature. The normal childhood sicknesses were taken much harder by Phillip and Friday; and, as a result, they never seemed to completely grow up to the size, nor acquire the confidence that the others had.

By the time Boies started at the Protestant Episcopal Academy, Dr. and Mrs. Penrose began to map out the balance of their educational program. Since Hannah had family who had gone to Harvard, she leaned toward sending the boys there. Even ten-year-old Speck understood this. When they got word of this idea, the boys had little or no resistance because they knew the respect a Harvard man commanded, and living as far away as Boston would afford them an opportunity to give vent to their impulses of raising hell — something that would most certainly encounter parental prohibition at home in the City of Brotherly Love.

CHAPTER III
THE PENROSE BOYS AT HARVARD

It was Hannah Penrose who decided that their sons would be Harvard men. She thought, if it was good enough for the Boieses and Hubbards, it certainly would be for her sons. Of course, Hannah made sure there was no mistake about the fact that Dr. Penrose would have to finalize the decision, which he did with great fanfare and ceremony.

The boys, in turn, were taken out of Episcopal Academy and turned over to a private tutor, one of whom was William S. Poney, in preparation for Harvard. By the time Boies was ready to enter Harvard in 1877, he was not yet seventeen, weighed over two hundred pounds, stood six feet, four inches in height, and had wavy black hair and steady black eyes that accentuated the insolent set of his mouth. His overbalanced poise and self-esteem gave him an exalted air. He openly displayed a feeling of contempt toward the world and its puny inhabitants. Because of Boies' lazy, lackadaisical attitude toward his studies, Tal, over a year his junior, caught up with him scholastically, so both boys were scheduled to enter Harvard at the same time.

The parents made several visits to Cambridge, Massachusetts, and on two occasions conferred with the Harvard president, Dr. Charles W. Elliot. Commenting on these two interviews Dr. Elliot said, "They impressed me very much with their intelligence and solicitude with regard to the education of their boys. Although neither of their families had had any connection with Harvard University, unless possibly Mrs. Penrose in William Hubbard, 1642, both were bent on educating all their sons at Harvard College. I thought at one time Dr. Penrose selected Harvard College because of the interest he took in reforms in the Harvard Medical School, which took place between 1870 and 1875." Evidently Dr. Elliot did not discuss William Hubbard with the Penroses.

As the Penroses prepared to enroll their boys in the fall of 1877, they made some more important long-range plans. All six of their sons would definitely go through college in precisely the same pattern. The Penroses studied the college dormitories and their management and made themselves acquainted with the mode of life of Harvard students in general.

Hannah Penrose was anxious that her sons associate with the right people and eschew all improper contacts. She decided that she would not trust her boys alone to find their way about such a strange place as Boston. So Dr. Penrose bought a house on Gerry Street, near the Harvard Yard, following their belief that their well-born, young, blue bloods would not mix too freely with ordinary undergraduates. Sarah Beck, the boys' maiden cousin of somewhat advanced years, was installed as a housemother. When Boies and Tal were told that they were to live in a private Penrose dormitory and that Cousin Sarah would be there to supervise their conduct and morals, they protested, but to no avail.

The decision was irrevocable. They had never had any real freedom anyway, so after the initial shock they did not consider this program too harsh.

To further assure themselves that their boys would observe regular habits and remain gentlemen at all times, Dr. and Mrs. Penrose presented them with these eleven written rules before they entered school in October, 1877:

1. Miss Beck, possessing the affection and entire confidence of your father and mother, should be treated with the greatest respect, and her advice and suggestions should be received respectfully, and as a rule, followed.

2. Be particular and neat about your dress — keep your shoes clean and well blackened — wash hands, brush hair before going to meals, and endeavor always to be ready when the meal is served.

3. Never retire for the night after studying all evening, without first going to Miss Beck, having a little social conversation with her, and bidding her goodnight.

4. Let ten o'clock be your latest hour for going to bed, if possible go earlier, never later.

5. Twice a week take a soap bath — the best time for this bath, I think, would be before going to bed.

6. Take from two to three hours, daily, active exercise — about five days in the week. Go to the gymnasium for about an hour a day. While there, never attempt to excel or do any difficult or unusual feat. Walk an hour or two every day and box daily or frequently.

7. Be careful in changing wet shoes, stockings, and clothes. Put on winter flannels when the thermometer gets about thirty-two degrees. At all times, accept Miss Beck's advice about clothing.

8. Avoid constipation of the bowels by exercising, bathing, eating fruits and vegetables, and especially, by taking some fixed time, as after breakfast, invariable, to give them the opportunity to act. If two days pass without a movement, take an Anderson's pill at bed time, or two teaspoonfuls (more or less) of crab orchard salt in a whole tumbler of water immediately on rising in the morning.

9. Always go to church on Sunday morning — preferably, with Miss Beck. If not with her, go to the college chapel.

10. When invited out to dinner or tea be careful about dress, etc. If offered wine or cigars, quietly decline by saying you never smoke or use wine, and, at all times, give the same answer, no matter where or by whom offered.

11. Form at first, no intimacies — afterwards, only with quiet, hard working students. Avoid all "swell" fellows. And, by all means, join no secret society or club until the sophomore or junior year.

Presumably, the rules were read and accepted by the boys before they entered college.

Sarah Beck, who had a very kindly disposition, felt great responsibility for her younger cousins. In his memoirs, Dick Penrose wrote, "She had all of the pride and prejudices of a descendant of those who landed at Plymouth Rock in the earlier colonial days of Massachusetts." It wasn't long before a chance acquaintance of Boies was invited into the Gerry Street home of the boys, much to the annoyance of Cousin Sarah. But there was nothing she could do about it. The number increased. Hilarious sessions became common, and according to Boies' predictions, Sarah was shown "some great times."

Boies' attitude toward Harvard can best be told by his comparison of the school to a "first class dime museum." He considered the professors "mummified" and lacking in imagination. He told Tal, "the faculty got their jobs years ago, set in motion what ideas they had at the time, then ossified." When asked about one of his classmates by the name of Ted Roosevelt, Boies dubbed him "a conceited ass" and a "cock-eyed little runt." Because of Boies' well-known opinionated attitude and his arrogant personality, he was ostracized by most of the students, and during the greater part of his four years at college he was merely ignored by the leaders.

Meantime, serious-minded Dick Penrose had finished his preparation for Harvard under a tutor in Philadelphia and passed his final examinations in 1880 at the age of sixteen. Later that year, fourteen-year-old Speck was placed under the same tutor. Dr. and Mrs. Penrose could not bear the embarrassment that would be theirs if one of their offspring failed to pass the entrance examination for Harvard.

In the fall of 1880, the Penrose clan grew to three at Harvard when Dick moved in with Boies and Tal on Gerry Street. From his very first day at school, Dick proved to have the same caliber of intelligence as his older brothers. And, in addition to being inherently bright, he went a step further by becoming a member of Harvard's famous rowing team, the Crimson Crew. While his three older brothers were pursuing their education in Cambridge, Speck was being tutored to get through the Episcopal Academy with good enough grades to be able to follow their path to Harvard.

On a cold March afternoon in 1881, and on the servants' day off, Dr. Penrose had taken Phillip and Friday to the country. Speck was alone in the big house on Spruce Street with his mother, who had been sick with pneumonia, though considered well on the way to full recovery. Suddenly she started coughing, then gagged. Panicked, Speck did not know what to do or where to go for help. Hannah Penrose died before help arrived or anyone in the family returned. The terror, grief, and aloneness was all that Speck could bear.

Mrs. Penrose's death was totally unexpected. She would have been forty-seven the following day. Speck was then fifteen-and-a-half years old. The emotional impact of this tragic event would leave a lasting scar on him. The rest of the family took this loss particularly hard also. Although she had been somewhat cold and detached from the boys, Hannah Penrose was the only feminine member of the household, sharing her particular type of love with all her men. Destroying a vital part of each surviving member of the family, Hannah's death hurt them all equally.

Two months after Hannah Penrose's death, her two oldest sons graduated from Harvard with highest honors. Nineteen-year-old Tal finished first in a class of 200; Boies, second.

Tal was positive about his future aspirations. He wanted to follow in his father's footsteps and become a doctor. Conscientious, hard work agreed with Tal. He liked to be busy in something useful. His straightforward nature and strong-willed desire to pursue any effort with great determination made medicine a natural profession for him. To top it off, his good looks and even temper automatically made him popular in any medical group.

Boies' studies in law and politics at Harvard had ended up with a class oratory about Martin Van Buren, an assignment that piqued his interest in politics so much that after graduating he plunged into law and the political arena in his own city. Although it was not by design, he followed the pattern established by Theodore Roosevelt, who graduated from Harvard a year before he did and headed straight for a political career in the famous "Silk Stocking" district of upper-east-side Manhattan.

It was destined that Boies was to become that which carried the utmost in respectability and prestige, a Philadelphia lawyer. Accordingly, it was arranged for him to serve his apprenticeship by studying law in the offices of one of the leading firms in Philadelphia, Wayne MacVeagh & George Bispham. MacVeagh was Attorney General in President Garfield's cabinet.

Meanwhile, back at Harvard, Dick did not think that keeping the Gerry Street house going for one student seemed worthwhile. Tal had gone back to Philadelphia for a while before continuing work on his PhD at Harvard. So Dick got rooms nearby on Appian Way and left the house for the use and comfort of Cousin Sarah, who had taken care of it and the boys so efficiently for over four years. She was allowed to have the house as a residence for herself and her sister for the rest of her life.

In the fall of 1882, Speck entered Harvard at the age of sixteen. He resolved to emulate his three older brothers in scholastic attainment and campus activity. But from the beginning, it was evident that he would have a rough time even getting passing grades. So Dick found a tutor for him.

By association with Dick, Speck would have gained a great deal, since his brother was an excellent and conscientious student. Dick was also well liked by most of the professors. Sometimes he used this popularity with them to help his younger brother. Rhetoric, calculus, French, Greek and English literature were some of the courses taken by the ambitious Penroses. Speck found each one of his learning experiences at Harvard an almost insurmountable obstacle. For instance, Goldsmith's *Essays*, deQuincey's *Caesar*, and Mignet's *French Revolution* could be breezed through by Dick, but Speck stumbled and struggled through every chapter.

Dr. Penrose and his sons corresponded weekly. Instead of seeking a suitable replacement for the mother of his sons, Dr. Penrose elected to raise them himself. The death of his wife had softened him. He not only provided sound fatherly advice and counseling but also a regular supply of butter and mutton, items which were at a premium. Dr. Penrose also periodically sent preserves, which Speck described in a letter as "bully."

After a fierce Boston snowstorm in early December of 1882, Speck helped shovel the foot-deep snow off the football field where the Harvard and Yale freshmen clashed in a tie game. Afterwards he sat down in his room on Appian Way and gave this account to his father on his scholastic standings:

> I have another examination in geometry next Thursday. I will try to pass it better than I did my last geometry examination since Professor Byerly said I did not pass very well. The Greek class has been divided into five sections according to the marks the fellows got last examination. I am in the fourth section — I passed well enough to be in the second but (professor) Dyer, the Greek fellow didn't agree with me, and this is the reason I am in the fourth. The Latin fellow has not

Speck and four brothers are shown here in a formal setting with their father. From left to right are Boies, Spencer, Phillip, Dr. Penrose, Charles and Richard or R.A.F., Jr. Missing is Francis Penrose.
Courtesy, Pikes Peak Library District.

told us our marks — I will ask him next recitation if
he will let me (know) how I passed.

Speck's failure to measure up to his brothers was a bitter disappointment to Dr. Penrose. Although he tried hard, as
Dick indicated in his letters to the doctor, Speck still did not
bring home the results. Each minor incident with his father
became an episode in a program bent on failure and disgrace
to the family.

For many years now, the incidents had been accumu-
lating and the conflict had been building up between Dr.
Penrose and Speck. The under-the-surface differences seemed to
intensify. Boies' differences with Dr. Penrose could be excused
by his brilliant scholastic record and immediate skyrocketing
success in the legal profession. But there was no equalizer for
Speck. Although Speck loved and respected his father, Dr. Penrose was openly disappointed, not only in Speck's inability to
follow the steps of his older brothers, but his attitude of resistance toward the rules set down by his parents.

Dr. Penrose was a pragmatic parent. He had an unexpected side that no one saw but the boys. He strongly advo-
cated an academic education, but he also believed that the
boys should know about wine, women and song, despite
rule number ten of the "eleven written rules" on abstinence.
He insisted that his offspring become versed in the wiles by
which women enticed men into their nets, and that they
learn how to wriggle free when enslavement by females
threatened. For this training, when the boys were home from
school, he directed them to the dives along the Schuylkill
River where young Philadelphians had sown their wild oats
for several generations. This was a parent-sponsored activity
Speck savored.

Everything Speck attempted seemed doomed to being misunderstood or an out-and-out failure. While he was trying out for the Harvard Crimson Crew team, he wound up ingloriously in the infirmary after seriously damaging the retina of his left eye. It happened when the edge of an oar flipped up and hit him as he tried to lift a shell from the Charles River. After some medical attention he did, however, gradually regain his sight. This unsuccessful effort to win a place beside his brother Dick on the Crimson Crew was a devastating blow to his ego.

In his search for distinction at Harvard, Speck did manage to break one record. He drank a pitcher of beer in thirty-seven seconds. This fete won him admiration among the beer drinkers, but slowed him down considerably with his studies, which already needed far more of his attention. Speck was sensitive to criticism by his contemporaries and quickly challenged any adversary to a fight. Through these aggravated circumstances, which began in the back streets of Philadelphia, Speck became experienced in fist fighting. This was one thing he seemed to do well, so he decided to make an exerted attempt to further excel in it by taking lessons. He rationalized that his parents had included this activity as a suggested form of exercise in their eleven written rules. Since there were no instructors in the art of prize fighting on the Harvard campus, Speck sought out his own expert in the city of Boston and started taking lessons at twenty-five cents a piece from a big, black pugilist, "who teaches tricky ways of knocking fellows down."

So, while Dick was reading the life of Charles James Fox in German, and making crystal of ferrous sulfate, Speck was sharpening up his right hook and putting the finishing touches on his left jab with a professional boxer. He then usually relaxed from this routine in one of Boston's local gin mills in the presence and comfort of a lady of questionable background.

Speck felt inferior to his brothers socially and intellectually. For example, they were good dancers and at ease with socially acceptable girls, while Speck was a horrible dancer and hopelessly inept at social chitchat. It was evident that Speck would never make it through college without the tutors hired by Dick and paid for by Dr. Penrose. "I don't think he could do much without Howell," wrote Dick to his father about Speck's chief tutor. Then he went on to give an accounting of their expenses for hiring him and others on Speck's behalf.

In a letter to his father Dick said, "Howell has been all evening with Speck tutoring him for his examinations. I guess he will get through all right as he has lately begun to make a big brace."

For Christmas, the Penrose boys usually came home to Philadelphia on a train that "leaves Boston at 10:30 p.m. and which could get us to Philadelphia in time for breakfast." Around Christmas time in 1883, Boies was admitted to the bar in Pennsylvania and at once began practice as a member of Page, Allison & Penrose.

Friday entered Harvard in 1884. While eighteen-year-old Speck plugged along at his studies and boxing lessons and Friday got himself established in school, in between bouts with colds and sleepless nights, Dick became stroke of the championship Crimson Crew. At the end of the year, Dick graduated summa cum laude in geology and qualified for his Phi Beta Kappa key. At the same time Tal performed an outstanding fete; he won two post graduate degrees, his PhD at Harvard and an MD at the University of

Pennsylvania. Meanwhile, Boies fulfilled the first step in his quest for a prominent place in public life. He was elected to the state legislature in Pennsylvania, a paradoxical accomplishment considering his popularity at Harvard. In 1885, during his second year at Harvard, Friday came down with a brain fever and returned to Philadelphia for treatment closer to his father's supervision. He was an invalid thereafter. This left Speck and Dick alone at Harvard to carry the family banner. Dick stayed on to get his MA and PhD in geology.

In 1886, Speck, at age twenty, barely squeaked through for a bachelor's degree in engineering.

CHAPTER IV

A Father's
Distrust

After graduation Speck was not able to settle down to anything that resembled a successful career. On the surface, however, he appeared to be an individual who could handle just about anything. He had developed into a good looking, tall, solidly-built young man with dark wavy hair and the blue eyes and perfect profile of his family. He had an alertness and a decidedly masculine and positive manner that instantly earned most men's respect. Although ill-at-ease among the high-bred social set, he possessed a remarkable lopsided grin that was devastating to women.

Dr. Penrose, with his influence, arranged to have one of the city's leading banks, the Girard Company, take Speck in — probably with the secret hope that one day he would be its president. But Speck was not interested. At twenty-one, a free wheeling, non-conformist, he believed deeply in his own personal liberty. He had become intimidated by Dr. Penrose's cold realism and rigid standards of discipline. As a result of a rather complicated psyche acquired from a sterile childhood home life, the situation surrounding the untimely death of his mother, his extremely successful brothers, and his father's hard attitude — he had nourished a burning, fundamental urge to get rich ... on his own.

Although Speck had been unable to match the out-standing records of his brothers, already launched on brilliant careers in politics, medicine and geology, he still loved them and sought their advice. Subconsciously he felt the same way about his father, but as he observed Dr. Penrose's evident pride in the manner in which the three older boys had set out on their successful lives, he became conscious of his father's indifferent attitude toward him. After all, he did have the identical opportunities as his brothers, including an education at Harvard. Perhaps this is why Speck turned his back on Philadelphia and the social status he had inherited and became the maverick of the family.

Early in 1888, this twenty-two-year-old rowdy, restless, black sheep of the aristocratic Penrose family, who seemed destined to fill the role of a ne'er-do-well, decided to head for the great undeveloped West with a $2,000 stake from his father.

This was the time when adventurous men and eastern capital began to explore the limitless possibilities to be found in the vast region between the Midwestern plains and the Pacific. It had been almost twenty-five years since the agony of the Civil War. The northern industrial states were in the midst of a recovery with a great deal of serious concentration focused on the West.

Spurred on by his brother Dick, Speck himself had only a vague notion of where he wanted to go or what he wanted to do. Of course, in addition to the rational, well-thought-out suggestions he got from Dick, he had read the popular and current western adventure stories, often the fabrication of an imaginative writer who had not left the shores of New Jersey.

Armed with this dubious information, Speck headed West, as Horace Greeley directed, with dreams of glory.

After a brief venture in the Yaque Indian country of Mexico searching for gold, he landed in dry, desolate Las Cruces, New Mexico, as the partner of W.E. Laurence in a wholesale and retail dealership in fruits, vegetables, hay, grain, coal, lime, agricultural implements, stoves, etc. The letterhead of the operation bore the name "Messila Valley Fruit and Produce Company."

At first, the bright yellow and red countryside, splashed with the radiant rays of the hot southwestern sun and the dark Spanish-speaking natives, provided an exciting and intriguing adventure. But it soon wore thin.

Speck worked hard under adverse conditions. The New Mexico sun seemed to get hotter and hotter, lugging his produce became heavier and heavier, and his partner's disposition became less and less palatable. Furthermore, he had little or no communication with the customers, most of whom were Mexicans who could not speak English. This was, he thought, hardly the calling for a Philadelphia blue blood and Harvard man.

On December 2, 1888, Dick wrote to his father from Mineola Wood County, Texas, saying that he planned to go out to Las Cruces to see his brother. Dr. Penrose's paternal interest in the welfare of Speck is reflected in the fact that he wanted to reimburse Dick for his expenses to New Mexico to see Speck. However, this was interpreted by Speck as distrust from his father on his ability to succeed.

Dick, who was conducting geological surveys in Texas and Arkansas, kept in close contact with Speck. In a letter dated January 13, 1889, outlining his feelings toward Speck's situation in New Mexico, Dick described Las Cruces as a "wretched hole." He went on to explain how the land was dependent on irrigation canals, and how Congress had appropriated $100,000 for investigating the irrigation question in the Southwest, but how the canals were "in the hands of a lot of Americanized Mexicans, who let the irrigation improvements go to the devil and pocket the money."

He continued.

> I cannot see how Las Cruces would ever be a great center for anything but fruit and produce of the surrounding farms. The products of the country to the south of it would go to El Paso, those of the country to the north would go to Santa Fe, Albuquerque and other places nearer the markets. To the east and west of Las Cruces are deserts and mountains — many of which would be impossible to irrigate. Consequently, Cruces is shut off on the east and west by deserts and mountains and on the north and south by large railroad centers, which will take all possible trade from it. Of course, the mining interests in the mountains near Cruces may sometime be important as bringing trade to the town, but these are very uncertain things to count on.

In March of 1889, the youngest Penrose son, Phillip, came down with malaria. Speck returned to Philadelphia where he and his father, Tal, and Boies administered to Phillip's needs.

During this period, Speck made frequent trips back and forth between Las Cruces and Philadelphia, and he periodically stopped off in Austin, Texas, to visit Dick who had set up temporary headquarters there. On one such trip, just after Phillip was stricken, Speck and Dick came to an agreement with Professor Mill, one of Dick's geological colleagues, about a venture into the cement business. Speck was to settle his business in Las Cruces as soon as possible and return to Austin from where he and Mill would journey to Dallas to locate a site and take an option on the land for their proposed cement works. They would then write a prospectus and get the capital. At the time, Dallas was a prosperous and fast-growing town of 50,000, and the greatest railroad center in the state.

After the decision to relocate was final, Speck wasted no time in disposing of his New Mexico commission business for $2,000.

Back in Austin, Dick simply substituted Speck's name for his own so his brother would get a share of the promoter's profits as described in the prospectus. In a letter to his father, Dick wrote:

> I have entire confidence in Speck's ability to work the thing. The nerve and energy that he has shown in working against obstacles in Las Cruces prove what he could do if he had a fair show. He has worked as hard as any man could work and has had to contend with a lot of damned suckers who would have discouraged most men from doing anything.

Finally, all of the details on the cement scheme were worked out, but Speck became apathetic and the deal never culminated. This left Speck in a state of limbo — not a western businessman any longer, and certainly not a full-time resident of Philadelphia.

The following year, Speck left the City of Brotherly Love to take another sojourn out West where he discovered what he thought was a sure thing — a land deal in Utah. Not too far from Salt Lake City the Ute Indian reservation was being parceled off by the government to private industry. Speck considered the land valuable property and it was confirmed by Dick, who, by the nature of his strong, almost worshipful, brotherly love, still wanted to help Speck even after his sudden apathy toward the Dallas cement deal.

Dick Penrose's feelings toward his younger, twenty-four-year-old brother are best illustrated by this passage in a letter he wrote to his father on June 19, 1890.

> I have had several letters from Speck lately. He seems much encouraged about the prospects of the reservation being opened and I think he is on the track of a big thing. He deserves to succeed, as he is working hard and is a man of nerve. I wish I could be in Utah with him.

Unfortunately, the William Henry Harrison administration had second thoughts about selling the Indian land in Utah and the deal fell through, although Speck did have some good claims outside the reservation on which he purportedly made some money. Once more, however, Speck was met with failure, frustration, and a dim future without any goals.

Dick Penrose, in his capacity as a geologist and mining consultant, had visited Colorado several times and suggested that Speck try his luck there. The hot springs of Colorado drew Dick's attention as a possible investment for the development of a resort vacationland. In Glenwood Springs, for instance, there were any number of tourists drawn to the area because of its natural mineral baths and hot springs.

> ...take a look at those hot springs in Colorado. I saw them when the ground was covered by snow.

They impressed me as being a very valuable thing. They are on the western slope of the main range of the Rocky Mountains and in as beautiful a position as there is in Colorado. If they could be boomed as Hot Springs, Arkansas has been, they ought to be a big thing.

He was writing from Little Rock and obviously had been impressed by the hot springs there.

Again, the deal was never made because no desirable land was available and Speck eventually lost interest.

Speck's next venture was again one that was sparked by Dick. In the sedate little community of Colorado Springs was a boyhood chum of Speck's, Charles L. Tutt, who came there in 1884 from Philadelphia and had developed a meager real estate and insurance business. Speck had lost touch with Charles after his father, Dr. Tutt, had died. What Speck did not know was that Charles had to go to work before he finished high school.

Dick visited Tutt in Colorado Springs and they agreed to write Speck separately urging him to come to this part of Colorado. Dick wrote of the prospects of finding gold in the Cripple Creek district near Colorado Springs, while Tutt extolled the excellent climate, cricket games, polo balls, "the beautiful girls of Colorado and the most adequate bar at Cheyenne Mountain Country Club."

It has never really been known which argument paid off, but it would be a calculated guess that it was the latter. At any rate, Speck decided to go to Colorado Springs.

CHAPTER V
KNUCKLING DOWN

It was Thanksgiving in 1892 when Dick Penrose wrote to Charles Tutt about Speck's decision to come to Colorado Springs. At the time Dick was in Pearce, Arizona, working for the Pearce Copper Mining Company. Speck had just visited him and the conversation had centered around two subjects — the November 17 marriage in Philadelphia of Katherene Drexel to their brother Tal, and, of course, Colorado Springs.

It took the letter a week to reach the C.L. Tutt Real Estate and Insurance Company offices on 14 East Pikes Peak Avenue in Colorado Springs. After Tutt read the letter, he hastened to get things ready for Speck's arrival. It had been almost twenty years ago that the twosome attended Philadelphia's Protestant Episcopal Academy together and their fathers were fellows in the medical profession.

On Saturday, December 10, twenty-seven-year-old Spencer Penrose, only five years out of Harvard and already a seasoned western adventurer, arrived at the Santa Fe depot in Colorado Springs with less than $100 in his wallet, which meant, by the standards of an eastern Ivy League aristocrat, that he was broke. The train Speck arrived on was loaded with passengers bound for Denver and the booming gold mining community of Cripple Creek. The air was electric with "gold fever" and few passengers were staying on in Colorado Springs.

It had been as early as 1858 that gold seekers headed west across the sweltering plains toward Colorado with the slogan "Pikes Peak or Bust" scrawled across the canvas coverings of their prairie schooners. Their destination was not particularly the immediate vicinity of the 14,110-foot-high mountain that Lieutenant Zebulon Montgomery Pike had discovered in 1806. They intended to comb the vast and rugged Rocky Mountains of Colorado for the precious metal. But Pikes Peak, a towering sentinel in central Colorado where the mountains meet the plains, was the most publicized mountain in the country, and the name lent itself to the slogan, which caught on quickly with all who were to make the somewhat perilous trek to the bonanza country.

There was something prophetic about the "Pikes Peak" battle cry of the gold-hungry pilgrims. They thought only of gold; but when the prospectors got to digging, they turned up silver, first at Central City in 1859, and quickly thereafter at Leadville, Aspen, Silverton, Creede, and many other areas. This silver boom contributed mightily to the building of the territory's economy. Many became rich like H.A.W. Tabor and "Leadville" Johnny Brown. Some remained to help build their communities with their wealth; others took their loot elsewhere. Now, over thirty years later, a whole new cycle had begun with big new strikes in Cripple Creek, Victor, Midway, Cameron, and Altman. But this time it was gold!

Tutt, who was at the station to meet Speck, did not find it difficult to spot him as he stepped off the train. The stately, good looking man in his late twenties stood erect and drew considerable attention as he strolled down the platform, gripping his bag with one hand and holding his Chesterfield coat with the other, oblivious to the cold. By this time, Speck was sporting a black, neatly-trimmed mustache that matched his wavy hair. He wore a western hat, English style riding boots, and breeches that he had acquired during his travels and had become accustomed to. He had a serious expression on his face that did not exactly exude friendliness.

Twenty-eight-year-old Charles Leaming Tutt stuck out as inordinately sober amidst this throng of raucous, gold-hungry men. Like Speck, he too was a descendant of distinguished American patriots like Lieutenant Charles Tutt, a member of General George Washington's staff, who was killed in the Battle of Brandywine during the American Revolution. At the depot, Tutt appeared the epitome of calmness. Slightly taller than Speck, he had a red stubble of whiskers and a full head of dark hair. He wore glasses and sported an uncomfortable-looking high collar and wide tie.

As the two met, they both beamed with warm smiles of camaraderie that had begun in childhood. Speck gazed at the mountains west of the city and remarked on the view to his friend. Since it was winter, almost the entire range was white with snow. Pikes Peak easily dominated the horizon as it soared magnificently into the cloudless blue sky. Surprisingly, the farther away one got from the mountain, the bigger it appeared. The range extended as far south and north as the eye could see, creating the phenomenon of a barrier suddenly jutting up from the floor of the eastern plains.

They walked past the puffing steam engine as it started to pull out toward Denver with only three cars on the continuation of the northern spur of the main Santa Fe east-west route. Both men climbed into Tutt's one-horse buggy and headed for his office on East Pikes Peak Avenue.

Tutt then started answering Speck's questions about his city. He pointed out that before General William Jackson Palmer settled the area in 1871, no one lived there but rattlesnakes, prairie dogs, and assorted rodents. Palmer, also a Philadelphia aristocrat, had recruited a bunch of kids for a cavalry outfit at the beginning of the Civil War, and his distinguished record speaks for itself. After the war, Palmer was discharged a brigadier general at the ripe old age of thirty. He came to the area looking for a north-south railroad route that would run from Canada to South America through Denver and Colorado Springs.

General Palmer first rode past Pikes Peak the night of July 26, 1869, atop a Concord coach, wrapped in blankets to help ward off a thunderstorm. He was exhilarated and thrilled by all he saw. So impressed by the excellent climate and natural beauty of the Pikes Peak region, he founded the town of "Fountain Colony" in 1871 at the eastern base of the peak. This later became known as Colorado Springs. He built the railroad too — the Denver & Rio Grande. By 1890 the area had become a sedate center of culture.

At Tutt's one-room office, Penrose browsed around briefly as Tutt shuffled a few papers. Then Speck asked his friend where he could buy him a drink. With this question Tutt again launched into another tale. When Palmer laid out the town, he would only sell lots to persons of "good character and strict temperance habits." So the city was quite dry. Consequently, in order to get a drink they would have to go a few miles south outside the city limits to the Cheyenne Mountain Country Club where Tutt was a member.

Charles went on with his commentary. The British influence was strong in Colorado Springs since they were among the earliest settlers, so much so, the city was known as "Little London."

As described by a western newspaper columnist:

The British came early, including many playboys with that flair for roving the world so inherent in the English — bringing with them a caravan of animals, cronies and ladies. The London paper carried advertisements in the 1870s advising the gentry of a fabulous safari in Colorado where game like bison and grizzly abounded. The English brought the blue blood cattle most of which was driven to the lush grasslands of Colorado from Texas...Herefords, Ayashires, Jerseys, Alderneys, Devones and Galloways.

London's business circles were besieged by promoters who sold sure things in Colorado's fabled gold and silver mines. A great deal of English capital went into the mines — some of it lost and some to make wealthy men of investors who never set foot in Colorado. The British brought tradition, arts, culture. When the gold camps became cities, hungry for refinement and entertainment, the state's hallowed boards were trod by theatrical and singing stars and artists and lecturers. General Palmer journeyed often to London to promote money for his city and for the railroad he envisioned. The British were truly the keystone of high society until money finally broke the barriers.

The climate had also drawn several thousand, many wealthy and well educated, who came there searching for a cure of "consumption." There were rich and poor alike — the merchants, the service crowd, and workers in small factories along the railroad tracks west of town. The population tripled between 1880 and 1890. In 1891, there were 15,000 who called Colorado Springs their home.

It was ironic that Palmer, Tutt, and Penrose should all be Philadelphians. Tutt arrived eight years previously, after a $500 misadventure into business in North Platte, Nebraska — a frail young man, longing for a job that would bring color to his face and add strength to his physique. Since his father died when he was in his teens, he had to go to work before finishing high school. He bought a ranch in the Black Forest area, eighteen miles north of Colorado Springs, where he worked for three exhausting years. In 1887, he married Josephine Thayer, daughter of Martin Russell Thayer, a prominent Philadelphia jurist. She did not fancy being a rancher's wife, so once married, Tutt sold out and moved into town to sell real estate and insurance.

As Penrose and Tutt left the office, Tutt pointed out the largest building in the district, the Antlers Hotel built by Palmer and where President Harrison had stopped last May. Situated on a four-acre estate, the five-story Antlers Hotel featured lounges, a dining room, a billiard room, a card room, children's and servant's dining rooms, guest rooms and suites, a kitchen, pantries, a baker shop, and Turkish baths.

Tutt's horse trotted east to Nevada Avenue, then south into Broadmoor. As they rode, Tutt pointed out that the city's homes and lawns were protected by tall cottonwoods, maples, elms and lindens; that there were many big homes of Tudor design with stables in the rear for fine horses and carriages; and, in the modest class, there were comfortable, peak-roofed cottages on neat fifty-foot lots. It was a perfect

Christmas card setting, Speck thought. Evergreens and snow covered mountains; wreath-decorated windows and doors. Everyone was bundled up against the elements, and the crisp air seemed to put a cheerful, liveliness to their step that added to the holiday spirit.

The Tutt buggy passed by the famous Colorado School for Deaf and Blind, through Dorchester Park, and by the Broadmoor Dairy Farm. When the rig reached the point on Lake Avenue, which was being lined with trolley tracks, opposite the circular driveway of the Cheyenne Mountain Country Club, Tutt identified a large building at the end of the street, three blocks west, as the Pourtales' Casino, and pointed to the polo fields south of the club.

As a footman took charge of the horse, Tutt explained in a low voice to Speck that this was a pretty reserved group at the club. He gave him an example of the attitude that existed in certain quarters. There had been a silver boom in Leadville, a rip-roaring, wide-open town over the mountains 100 miles west as the crow flies. Some of the Colorado Springs puritans seemed to resent even being in the same state with such a place. Tutt said there was no telling what they would think when Cripple Creek, just over the mountain and in the same county, got going full blast with its gold discovery.

It was mid-afternoon when the two entered the club. Luncheon had been served in the customary leisurely atmosphere. Although the sun beamed brightly, one could see the breath of the finely dressed members and guests who waited for their carriages, buggies, and saddled horses on the outside veranda of the club.

Two days before, the countryside had been blanketed with snow, but there remained only a few spots of white in places shaded from the intense Colorado sun. Thus far, the winter had been pleasantly mild in this part of Colorado. So mild, in fact, that it became a part of most conversations along with the forthcoming New York World's Fair, the nation's teetering economic situation, and the gold seekers who were swarming on the other side of Pikes Peak.

In the game room a dozen gentlemen were engaged in roulette, baccarat, and poker, backed up by an assortment of kibitzers. And a large green billiard table in another room was the focal point for four players and a few spectators. Several members were reading in Queen Anne chairs in the front sitting room while a fire crackled in the over-sized fireplace. It was a comfortable, secure — even cozy — atmosphere that club members relished with a pardonable pride.

Tutt and Penrose checked their coats and hats, after which Penrose signed the guest book in a strong, forward-leaning hand. Speck seemed more than pleased to observe such an adequate well-furnished bar, with a brass foot-rail that extended from end to end and brass spittoons strategically located at each end. The floor was polished brick, and on the opposite side of the room were tables where several men sat nursing their drinks. A cash register on the back bar indicated that members could pay cash if they chose not to sign tabs. One bartender on duty was able to take care of the afternoon trade.

The two newest customers took a place near one end of the bar and ordered shots, with water on the side. They engaged in conversation slightly above a whisper. By this time, Speck had decided that this was the most beautiful spot he had ever seen, and he also discovered that the mile high elevation gave liquor an extra kick. Such a combination seemed almost too good to be true. Inasmuch as Speck Penrose had come to make a career in the Pikes Peak region, he was anxious to know what Charles, who had invited him here, had in mind. The pair was now working on drink number four. Occasionally, their conversation veered from the serious business of a career for Penrose to comments on minor happenings and persons at the club.

Suddenly two men in the midst of a heated argument burst into the bar. The larger and louder of the two was a stocky, well-dressed man perhaps thirty years old, who seemed to be disturbed as the result of the ridicule of one of his polo ponies by his adversary, a much smaller man. The big one ordered a drink as the argument continued. Tutt whispered to Speck that the large fellow was Harry McKeon, the hotshot on the polo team, and the little man was one of the earliest members of the club, Shiner Casement.

The antagonists continued their argument as the barkeeper cautioned them that their conduct was not becoming of club members. Round number five was brought to Tutt and Penrose while McKeon downed another. Casement continued his provocative verbal thrusts, displaying a Napoleonic air sometimes taken on by short men. Finally, at what appeared to be the peak of his excitement, McKeon stood up, pulling the little man with him; then he knocked Casement to the floor with considerable force. Although surprised and stunned, Casement was not seriously hurt, but fearing another blow laid still on the floor. A tense few moments followed as the dozen or more witnesses appeared shocked over having seen the first brawl in their sedate club. But this event was only a mild bolt of lightning signaling a terrific thunderclap.

Speck Penrose took the drink before him in one gulp, carefully put the glass down on the mahogany bar, and without a word to Tutt walked over to McKeon, now seated at the table. He lifted McKeon to his feet by the coat lapels then doubled up his fists. With a right and a left to McKeon's face, he sent the polo star reeling over the table. The blows were hard enough to send McKeon through the French doors that opened onto the veranda. He appeared to be out, completely. In the same deliberate manner, Penrose walked over to Shiner, leaned down and picked him up. Unsure of Speck's next move, the little man quickly took the offensive and grunted that he could settle his own arguments and that Speck should mind his own business. Then he backed away cautiously.

The stunned bystanders in the bar were joined by all others in the club, including cooks and waiters who were beginning to prepare Saturday night dinner. Two clubmen moved to help McKeon to his feet. A heavy, round-faced, bearded man, puffing furiously on a pipe, emerged from the club's office and asked Tutt in a deep, guttural Teutonic accent what was going on. Turning around to Speck, Tutt introduced him to the club founder, Count James de Pourtales. Tutt then told the Count to have the repairs made and put on his account; then, with Speck in tow, moved to exit.

All eyes were on the trio as they walked toward the entrance. Penrose apologized to Count Pourtales for his conduct. However, he made it clear that he considered McKeon in gross error. Casement was much too small a fellow to be picked on. He, himself, then offered to reimburse the club for the damages.

Tutt's embarrassment was only lessened by the fact that most of the members and guests who were at the club when he arrived had left. However, he reacted with considerable poise as he did not wish to give Speck the impression that he was terribly disturbed. Inwardly, Tutt suffered a sudden torment with the realization that his guest Spencer Penrose, a Philadelphia blue blood and Harvard man in town less than three hours, had so rudely trespassed the dignity of this exclusive sanctum by perpetrating a saloon-type brawl.

As the men rode away from the club, Tutt sensed that quiet Spencer Penrose was very contrite as he contemplated the impact of what he had done, so Charles turned their mood into a lighter vein as he laughed and said, "Colorado Springs now knows that Spencer Penrose has arrived."

CHAPTER VI

HAND SHAKE IN
LITTLE LONDON

After Tutt joked about the incident at the Cheyenne Mountain Country Club, Penrose was visibly relieved. Not wishing to discuss the embarrassing situation any further, Tutt quickly steered the conversation to Count Pourtales, whom Speck had just met under the rather awkward circumstances. Tutt described the Count as an honest-to-goodness German nobleman who came to this country to find some twelve percent mortgage money and to marry his beautiful cousin, now the Countess Berthe de Pourtales. She had been living in Florissant, a small ranching community a few miles west of Pikes Peak.

The Count had set out to develop the Broadmoor section on a grand scale. In 1885, he bought the Willcox dairy farm a short distance from the club, thinking to make it a very profitable business by introducing German agricultural methods. William J. Willcox was from a Philadelphia paper tycoon's family and a friend of Tutt's. After buying the Willcox farm, Count Pourtales acquired approximately 2,000 acres of ground around it with the idea of starting a big residential development. The trolley track on Lake Avenue in

Pikes Peak Library District
Special Collections

Gift of
El Pomar Investment Co.

Count James Pourtales is the German nobleman who founded the community of Broadmoor. In 1891 he built a casino where the present Broadmoor facility is located. Speck met Pourtales on his first day in Colorado Springs at the Cheyenne Mountain Country Club where Pourtales was the acting manager. After witnessing a physical encounter of the club's star polo player roughing up a smaller member, Speck stepped in and knocked the larger man to the floor. When the activity subsided Charles Tutt, a club member, and his guest, Speck, were politely escorted out of the club by Pourtales.

Courtesy, Pikes Peak Library District.

front of the club was evidence that he meant to do just that. He hoped to turn the casino into an American Monte Carlo. In back of the club, he built an artificial lake.

Though Pourtales was instrumental in establishing the Cheyenne Mountain Country Club, it actually was started in 1888, prior to his involvement, by a group of businessmen who soon lost interest. Finally, Pourtales stepped in and was the moving spirit in building it. The club had now been open for about sixteen months and the membership had soared to 250. The Count functioned as the de facto president who officiated in everything when he was around.

The sun had disappeared over Pikes Peak, and dusk had settled when the buggy again pulled up at the Tutt office to pick up Speck's luggage. They then headed toward the Tutt home at 611 North Weber Street for a family dinner and hopefully a much needed relaxed evening in congenial and comfortable surroundings.

The pair had been so occupied with other matters, including the hectic experience of the late afternoon, that hardly a mention had been made of the other members of the Tutt family whom Penrose had known slightly back east. Tutt's father, a skilled surgeon, Dr. Pendleton Tutt, died when Charles was only twelve years old. After the Episcopal Academy, Charles attended the Ury boarding school in the City of Brotherly Love but left school at seventeen to work as a clerk for the Pennsylvania Railroad. Once settled into family life in Colorado Springs, Tutt developed considerable foresight in his business activities with an acute mind and a keenness in practical matters.

The Tutt home on North Weber was a new gingerbread, two-story frame house, nicely furnished upstairs and down. In back of the house was a combination barn and buggy shed.

Penrose was heartened by the warmth of his reception in the Tutt household. Josephine Thayer Tutt greeted him graciously. She reminded Speck of their first introduction while he and Tutt were in boarding school and how disappointed they were that he could not come to their wedding.

The bachelor Penrose had never taken any interest in children — in fact, he was at times intolerant of their presence — but he took an immediate liking to Charles L. Tutt Jr. who would be four years old in another month. Formalities over, Charles escorted Speck to the upstairs guest room, suggesting that perhaps he might want to take a bath before dinner, which he did. While in his room dressing, he heard a knock at the door. The visitor turned out to be just what Speck hoped — Charles with a king-sized bourbon for each of them.

Sunday, December 11, was another bright but cold day in Colorado Springs. Mrs. Tutt was up early to prepare breakfast for her now enlarged family. The Tutts attended the Episcopal church regularly, so she suggested to Charles that perhaps Speck would like to go along, not knowing that he seldom went to church. Charles vetoed the proposal because, after what happened Saturday afternoon at the country club, he did not think Speck would wish to be seen in public so soon. Josephine had not been told of the fracas.

Both Speck and Charles anxiously perused all of the news columns in the Sunday morning issue of the *Daily Gazette* to see if the paper had covered the most spectacular event of the previous day in the greater Colorado Springs area. It had not.

In the perfectly relaxed atmosphere of the Tutt home, Charles and Speck got down to the serious business of planning the future, resuming where they left off the previous afternoon. Tutt explained that the real estate business in the Springs had not been too good due to the country's shaky economy that seemed to have most everyone scared. The one bright hope was Cripple Creek, according to Tutt, where the gold boom was just getting a good start. There had been a number of good strikes that had been made and several hundred mines in the district were being worked. Tutt considered the discovery of a gold mine an uncertain and risky business, but he thought a killing could be made in real estate. Tutt pointed out that people were flocking to Cripple Creek at the rate of many hundreds — perhaps thousands — each month. They were not only miners, prospectors, swashbuckling gamblers, and harlots, but people with money to set up the various kinds of businesses the area would need. There was plenty of vacant land to build on, Tutt insisted, and concluded that when he was up there a few days before, even the prostitutes did not have enough housing.

Tutt had operated a branch office in Pueblo, Colorado — about forty miles south — for three years. Now he wanted to establish another branch in Cripple Creek as soon as possible. As long as the gold boom lasted, he thought real estate could be a gold mine as well. He asked Speck to go up and manage that office, and assured him that terms profitable to both of them could be set up. At this point Speck, who had been listening quietly, said that although he was flattered, he would rather get part of the operation as a partner. Without batting an eye, Tutt announced that he was prepared to offer him one-half interest in the real estate business for $500 on the condition that he would go up and manage the office in Cripple Creek...the office of Tutt & Penrose.

Although Speck had about $100 in cash, he felt that he needed that to live on until he earned some income. So he asked if it would be all right if he pay the $500 for half interest in the business as soon as he began earning some money, and he offered a note for that amount with interest at the going rate. Since Tutt considered Speck's word as good as gold, he declined the note. He added that he hoped and expected this partnership would last a lifetime, not only in the real estate business but in any other venture in which they may become interested.

Tutt then told Speck about his other interest in Cripple Creek. He had filed a claim on a mine that was situated very close to the spot where Bob Womack, a roustabout cowboy, had discovered gold about eighteen months before in what became known as the El Paso Lode. It was located on the southwest slopes of Pikes Peak in a cow pasture called Cripple Creek. By this time, most of the gold seekers who had cried "Pikes Peak or Bust" thirty years earlier had either made their stake in silver, moved on to other mining areas, or died. It was Womack himself who had helped Tutt locate the claim.

Charles went on to say that the mine was near, of all places, "Poverty Gulch," and had the prophetic name of "Cash on Delivery." Since this property was surrounded by gold producing mines, Tutt felt that the chance of finding gold was as good, or nearly so, as any of the several hundred holes where digging was in progress. But like nearly all other prospectors, his problem was money with which to buy equipment and pay miners. Tutt then offered Speck one-sixteenth interest in the mine if he could raise $10,000.

Although Penrose had no idea of what he would use for money, the very thought of a gold mine electrified him. It was gold that had lured him to the far west; to Mexico and New Mexico and now Colorado. Tutt figured that if they could get the C.O.D. going, Speck could keep an eye on the mine while selling real estate. Tutt's plan was to incorporate the mining company and sell stock. It was kind of a slow process, but if $10,000 could be obtained they could get an early start. Speck indicated that he knew where the money was if he could only get a hold of it. He said he would write to his oldest brother Boies, now a member of the Pennsylvania State Senate. Speck thought that since Boies took care of the interests of the big money men in Harrisburg, if he did not have the money, he would surely know where to get it. Dr. Penrose had done very well with his investments and had the money, but Speck said he was too conservative to invest in gold mining stock. Furthermore, he was displeased when Speck took off for what he considered the "wild west" instead of pursuing a career in banking and investments in Philadelphia. Speck also thought that his father did not have much confidence in him. Later, in a fever of enthusiasm, Speck sat down and wrote Boies about the C.O.D. Mine, asking for $10,000 to take on a sixteenth share.

It was a buoyant pair of young businessmen that left the Tutt house Monday morning, December 12, 1892, bound for the office of C.L. Tutt & Co. Charles was secretly pleased that his Philadelphia boyhood pal had come to join him in his business ventures. He felt that Speck possessed the physical strength and energy to spark the new partnership into unprecedented success. Tutt had for some time felt that he needed something to stimulate himself, and now he had that something in the person of Speck Penrose.

The partners decided to put off the opening of their Cripple Creek office until after Christmas. Meantime, Speck's orientation in the real estate business would begin at once with ten easy lessons that would carry into the holidays. Now that their own plans had been solidified, Tutt was anxious to have his new associate get acquainted with the business and professional leaders of Colorado Springs. And Charles knew where to start with the introductions — General Palmer, of course. This undisputed kingpin of the sedate center of culture known as Colorado Springs received Penrose cordially. Palmer said he imagined that Speck had heard that the British had come to Colorado Springs in rather substantial numbers, apparently a favorite topic of conversation for the General. He concluded that he would like to see more entrepreneurs like Penrose and Tutt come to the area. Then he wished them both every success and offered them his cooperation.

Mr. and Mrs. Charles L. Tutt, being from a Philadelphia background of an acceptable social order, received invitations to the majority of Little London's (Colorado Springs' English nickname) "important" holiday parties, most of which were white tie and tails affairs featuring great pageantry and ceremony.

The Tutts wangled invitations for their friend to the elite's gayest parties: polo balls at the Antlers Hotel; cocktails at the El Paso Club, the oldest men's club west of Chicago; and private affairs given by the most prominent members of the social set. Speck tagged along to all of the gatherings they could possibly attend; and, at every opportunity, he and Tutt imbibed freely at the bar. That "obstreperous cuss," as Speck was referred to, fortunately made no repeat performances of the Cheyenne Mountain Country Club scene, now quite well known.

In addition to General Palmer, Speck met Dr. S.E. Solly, president of the El Paso Club and a skilled and articulate tuberculosis specialist who was largely responsible for establishing Colorado Springs as a center for the treatment and

General William Jackson Palmer, shown here in a portrait by Sir Hubert Von Herkomer, is a founder of Colorado Springs. In appreciation of his stalwart leadership, an equestrian statue of him now stands in Colorado Springs at the intersection of Platte and Nevada Avenues. Since Tutt was acquainted with the General, he arranged a meeting. The three Philadelphians chatted about the Tutt-Penrose plan of action. This was the beginning of a warm and productive relationship.

Courtesy, Pikes Peak Library District.

cure of the dreaded lung disease. Other notables he met included Henry Blackmer, a Massachusetts blue blood attorney who could "sweet talk" his way into almost any situation, and did; the Countess Berthe de Pourtales, celebrated beauty of her day and wife of the pipe-puffing founder of the Cheyenne Mountain Country Club; and Albert Eugene Carlton who came to Colorado the year before expecting to die of TB, but now looked healthy enough to outlive anyone.

Saying nothing was Speck's forte. As a result people thought him a good listener. Soon Speck intrigued more than the elderly gentlemen. His Barrymore-like profile, positive manner, swarthy figure, and, most of all, his quiet way, made him a target for every eligible young lady in the group. In truth, he was quite uncomfortable with the society ladies. But his quiet uneasiness created an impression of "the strong, silent type" which made him all the more appealing.

Josephine Thayer Tutt had an inherent driving desire to play cupid. She would not be happy until she had matched up her "single" friend with the "right" young lady. In this case, it was Nana Crosby, prima donna of Colorado Springs' socially prominent bachelorettes. Reluctant at first, Speck escorted Miss Crosby enough to actually establish an easy and comfortable rapport with her. The relationship reached a point that finally satisfied Josephine Tutt, who felt that she had truly fulfilled her womanly duties.

Speck had such wide-spread exposure in the community that he became the topic of many thoughts and conversations. Just who was this young Philadelphian who was so suddenly and prominently cast upon the scene of Little London? Was he a fortune hunter, rich playboy, or fraud? Perhaps he was the son of a wealthy eastern family who had finally decided to knuckle down and take roots in the west.

In 1894, this four-wheel, two-horse carriage won first place in the annual Colorado Springs Flower Parade. The rig was trimmed with smilax, geraniums, and sweet peas. It was owned by Mr. and Mrs. Charles L. Tutt, shown in the front seat with their guests in the back seat, Miss Nana Crosby (later the Marquise de Polignac) and Spencer Penrose. Denver Public Library. #1765

Speck's good looks, social graces, and keen interest in mining soon made him openly welcome and accepted by one of the most affluent social colonies between St. Louis and the west coast.

In the midst of all the social whirl, Speck received a wire from Boies in answer to his request for $10,000 to invest in the C.O.D. Mine.

STOP MAKING A FOOL OF YOURSELF. SEND-
ING YOU ONE HUNDRED-FIFTY DOLLARS
FOR YOUR FARE HOME.
BOIES

Speck showed this terse message to Tutt, then asked if it was all right with him to invest this $150 into the mine and pay off the rest as his earning permitted. Charles agreed, and the two men sealed the agreement with a firm and enthusiastic hand shake.

Speck and his new partner, Charles Leaming Tutt, looking over their agreement in 1892, which among other things, gave Speck the responsibility of managing their real estate holdings in Cripple Creek. Later this partnership, after a series of ups and downs, became an overwhelming success. It included a thriving real estate business, a productive gold mine, an expanding sampling and ore company, the largest reduction mill in the area, one of the most profitable copper mining ventures in history, and a myriad of other accomplishments.

Courtesy, Pikes Peak Library District.

CHAPTER VII
THE YOUNG GREENHORN

Speck's interest in the Cripple Creek area was shared by the whole country, not only because of the gold boom but as a result of the collapse of the silver industry. With the repeal of the Sherman Silver Purchase Act in 1893, Colorado, the nation's top silver producer, was left paralyzed. Many banks closed. Silver mining towns were being evacuated.

A Cripple Creek gold boom was inevitable, and when it boomed in 1891, it boomed with vengeance. What began with the '91 gold rush had now intensified with the collapse of silver. The rip-roaring mountain town of Cripple Creek, widely proclaimed as "The Largest Gold Camp on Earth," became known as the brightest spot in a country in the throes of the Silver Panic of 1893.

Besides Cripple Creek, in a rugged 400-square mile area later known as Teller County, there were twelve towns scattered about the western base of Colorado's famous Pikes Peak with populations ranging in size from 200 to 2,000. They included Victor, Goldfield, Cameron, Altman, Independence, Elkton, and Gillett. By this time, the estimated population in Cripple Creek itself had exploded to over 13,000, a long way from the 400 who were in this part of the Rocky Mountains at the end of 1891 when gold was first discovered there.

With the gold standard taking over, displaced hard-rock miners flocked to the area from defunct silver mining communities at a rate of over 500 a month. They hastily built ore houses, tipples, shafts, shacks, and other temporary-looking structures. By now gold production, in what became known as the "Crik," measured in the millions of dollars. In 1893, the transition had already begun from tent-and-shack town to metropolis, complete with crowded hotels, bustling bar rooms, and a crystal opera house.

The exodus from the silver camps brought newcomers to Cripple Creek over two wagon-road routes from Colorado Springs. The one used by the Cheyenne Mountain Stage was the road that skirted Pikes Peak on the south and was shorter by five miles than the more traveled Ute Pass highway through Manitou Springs on the north.

Penrose, accompanied by Tutt, took the Ute Pass road in Tutt's large-wheel Phaeton — a tough forty-four mile stretch for even the best of horses. Starting at dawn it, was an all-day drive. Although it was mid-winter, the many horse-drawn carriages, wagons, carts, and stage coaches that moved over the route kept it reasonably clear of snow. All of the precious metal mines in Colorado were in rugged, high mountain country, from 7,500 to more than 10,000 feet above sea level. The Cripple Creek mining district was the most rugged of them all. The road leading into Cripple Creek, for a stretch of ten miles to the north, had been drilled at many points along the rim of a gorge some 1,500 to 2,500 feet deep, the sides of which were vertical. A human or animal slipping off the edge of such a precipitous cliff would be allowed just that one mistake. These mountains were heavily timbered with not only pines and aspens, but other trees of various kinds, and shrubs amid grassy mounds — a beautiful breath-taking sight in the verdant spring, the summer, and the Indian summer autumn.

Finally, just after dark, the Tutt carriage came to a bluff above a community that nestled in a valley some 1,500 feet below. Thousands of chimneys discharged smoke from wood or coal stoves, and lights from kerosene lamps could be seen flickering through as many windows. A heavy cluster of lights, including electric street lamps, concentrated in a fairly sizable area immediately below, marked a rapidly-growing business district where another night of revelry was beginning. Tutt had seen it before, but to Speck Penrose it was a thrilling sight in the crisp, cold mountain air.

Once in town the weary travelers checked in at the Palace Hotel, Tutt having had the foresight to make reservations. They billeted the horses in Alonzo Welty's Stable. After washing up they reckoned as how a few shots of bourbon would go good before supper, and they proceeded accordingly. After looking in on a couple of gambling houses and a dance hall, the partners retired for a good night's rest.

Tutt and Penrose were up early on their first business day in Cripple Creek. When Penrose got his first daylight glimpse of his new home town, he was amazed. The mountains to the east, north and south were majestic; and on the west, the Sangre de Cristo range, buttressed by the Continental Divide, formed an imposing backdrop. Speck was amazed, too, that so much could have been built in two short years. The intensity of the digging for gold, with mines, large and small, popping out on every steep mountain slope, not only added to this amazement but sparked a determination within him to make the grade here in a big way.

Virtually all who came to Cripple Creek found work. Digging for gold was moving ahead at a feverish pace and towns were cropping up in many sections of the Cripple Creek mining district. Victor was six miles south and second in size to the Crik. Each one of the small camps had to have the routine services — stores, livery stables, coal and wood purveyors, apothecaries, hay, grain marts, boarding houses. In the non-essential class, saloons were bound to spring up as well as red-light districts, so even the scarlet women who came shared in the unique prosperity of the district.

The two newcomers made the rounds of several business places where Tutt had friends, all of whom were introduced to his new partner. They signed a lease for an office between Third and Fourth Streets on Bennett Avenue near the First National Bank in the heart of the business district. As Tutt and Penrose toured the streets of Cripple Creek to get acquainted with its real estate, the commodity in which they would be dealing, Penrose's Harvard engineering education suggested that the town had been platted in a crazy-quilt pattern, for the streets did not conform to the topography. Speck remarked that whoever laid out the town must have been drunk. Cripple Creek could never have had a baseball team. There just wasn't enough level ground to block out an infield, much less an outfield, without a lot of excavating; and the only excavating there was time for was up in the mines.

Tutt gave Penrose a brief history of the cow pasture that became Cripple Creek. In 1885, an eastern speculator named Phillip Ellsworth called on Bob Womack, the only one living in the area at the time, saying that he owned one-half interest in four, 160-acre homesteads for which he had paid $75,000, and which he found going to ruin. Womack intimated that he had paid too much for his interest,

In 1886, Bob Womack's strike at his Poverty Gulch Mine started what became the Cripple Creek gold boom. Following Womack were Jimmie Doyle and Jimmie Burns, firemen; and Winfield Scott Stratton, carpenter and cabinet maker — all from Colorado Springs — who staked their claims at the Portland and Independence Mines. These early prospectors paved the way for what would eventually lead to the creation of "The Largest Gold Camp on Earth."

Denver Public Library Western Collection. F22733

telling him that in 1876, the Womack family had acquired two of the four homesteads for $500 cash and two pigs. Upon hearing this, Ellsworth acquired full ownership of the homesteads by threatening his partners with prosecution for fraud. He then went to Denver where he met with young Horace Bennett, a senior partner in the real estate firm of Bennett and Myers. After considerable maneuvering, Ellsworth sold the whole works, land and what improvements there were, for $25,000 to Bennett and his partner Julius Myers. With a generous offer of $5,000 down and the balance "when you catch him," Bennett and Myers agreed, though Bennett had no faith in that district's gold potential and Myers thought of it as simply a great place to fish.

When gold became a reality, Bennett and Myers — still doubtful — reluctantly agreed to the platting of the northern, hilly half of what was called the Broken Box Ranch because it was too cruel a habitation for cattle. That became the town of Cripple Creek.

Thirty blocks divided into 766 lots (priced twenty-five dollars for inside lots and fifty dollars for corner lots) were hastily platted in the Bennett and Meyers Denver real estate office. Before filing the plat on November 6, 1891, the partners decided to name the principal streets. Bennett inscribed his name on the widest and most central of the east-west streets. Myers marked "Myers Avenue" on the first parallel street south of Bennett. They named Carr Avenue for George Carr, foreman of the Broken Box Ranch, Warren Avenue for a business tenant of the firm, and Eaton Avenue for Myers' brother-in-law. Five narrower north-south streets were given numerical designations beginning at the west end.

As the business district mushroomed, prostitutes began setting themselves up in business in various locations. City officials wanted the red-light district concentrated in one area. The best location was at the east end of Myers Avenue, beginning at Fifth Street, which was in the southeast corner of the business district. The parlor houses, two-story wooden structures, were on the north side of the street, with the cribs on the south side. Lucius Beebe described the Cripple Creek tenderloin district as the biggest in the West, except for Butte, Montana; and Marshall Sprague, the able Cripple Creek historian, referred to it as "one of the country's best-known red-light districts." However, Julius Myers, a puritanical soul, was terribly disturbed to have such a large and flourishing center of prostitution bear his name.

Speck Penrose on the other hand had seen enough of this place on his first full day to become consumed with enthusiasm. He fell in love with Cripple Creek.

After his first day of business Speck looked for relaxation, excitement, and whiskey in several saloons. He had become separated from Tutt when he sauntered into Johnnie Nolan's, which seemed to Speck to be the busiest and most interesting of the night spots. Patrons were playing poker, faro, and twenty-one. Wherever he went, the tall handsome, well-dressed Penrose was the cynosure of many eyes, both male and female. Undoubtedly he stuck out in the roughneck mountain crowd as a dude, attired in nicely tailored riding-breeches, $100 English boots, and a button-down vest topped off with a wide-brimmed western hat.

The young men in wing collars, pin-stripe suits, and bowler hats who were plentiful in some quarters made Penrose look like he had donned this "western" costume just for the occasion. Making sport of fleecing the young greenhorns was as popular a night-time activity for many of the tough miners just down from the sluices, as tampering with dance-hall girls for spicy favors.

As Speck stepped to the bar at Nolan's, two handsome gregarious patrons engaged him in conversation. They were Horace Devereux, a large hulky, well-dressed man about Speck's age who had gone to Princeton and had lived around New Jersey and Philadelphia all of his life, and pink-cheeked Harry Leonard, a New Yorker who had attended Columbia University.

Speck felt that he was obliged to tell his new-found friends that he was a Harvard man. He soon learned that Devereux had been a Princeton football star, class of 1881, and was a respected polo player. Leonard, a product of St. Mark's School as well as Columbia, was temporarily employed as a driver for the Cheyenne Mountain stage with plans to become an ordinary miner.

After a couple of rounds of get-acquainted drinks, Devereux suggested giving Speck a tour of the tenderloin. Speck said he had passed through it on his day of inspection, reserving a personal visit for a later time. The trio looked into the parlor houses on Myers Avenue. A most cordial welcome awaited them at each house, but they were merely sightseers this night. In the one-room cribs on the other side of the street, girls offered whatever they had to sell by lowering and raising their window shades.

Penrose lost no time in getting solidly into the real estate business. He and Tutt set up their office with what furniture and office equipment they could afford. Inasmuch as horse and buggy — or at least saddle — were essential to the operation of a sales organization, Speck looked for a horse. He finally found and bought for twenty-five dollars a beautiful white horse of Arabian ancestry — an equestrian aristocrat

The Tutt & Penrose building in Cripple Creek, circa 1890, was obviously a busy place as shown here. Speck in his trademark attire stands in front of the door, fifth from the left. The sign above reads "Real Estate, Mines and Mining Stocks".
Courtesy, Pikes Peak Library District

named "Rabbit" who soon was to be as familiar a sight in downtown Cripple Creek as Penrose himself.

Eventually profits started to roll in at the firm of Tutt & Penrose from the sale of placer lots and from expert promotion by Speck in the town of Gillett, a short distance from Cripple Creek. The firm was beginning to move property in the area. Penrose established himself early in the game as a hustler. Here is an advertisement he wrote for the *Cripple Creek Crusher* in March, 1893:

TUTT & PENROSE ARE RECORD BREAKERS
IN SELLING REAL ESTATE.
LIST YOUR PROPERTY WITH THEM AND
THEY WILL SELL IT
BEFORE YOU LEAVE THEIR OFFICE.

And another ad which appeared the same month:

BUY A BLOC OF LOTS
IN CRIPPLE CREEK
FROM TUTT & PENROSE AND
NET ENOUGH TO GO
TO THE WORLD'S FAIR.

The partners dabbled in almost everything. They built an office building and leased another. They bought and then leased the Myers Avenue building known as the Topic Dance Hall. Speck had to hire more sales and office help. Rent collections were his biggest problem.

Tutt and Penrose did not confine their Cripple Creek operations merely to real estate. With the boom in full bloom there was money to be made in mining stocks and property.

A full page ad in the *Cripple Creek Mining and Business Directory* read:

TUTT & PENROSE
REAL ESTATE AND MINES
MINING STOCKS
BOUGHT AND SOLD ON COMMISSION.
CORRESPONDENCE SOLICITED
335 BENNETT AVENUE
CRIPPLE CREEK, COLORADO

Another similar ad in an early-day mining directory listed Tutt & Penrose as "Financial Brokers" with offices in Cripple Creek and Colorado Springs. Still another ad listed a branch in Pueblo.

Penrose — with his penetrating blue eyes, near perfect features, and a clean-shaven face save for a small dark mustache that matched his dark wavy hair — became well known in the district. People noticed that his smile was not an easy smile, but one that he kept in check. He stood erect with a physique that could be used to illustrate any gentlemen's fashion book. His hands were large and yet had the delicateness of an artist.

The only part of his dress that showed anything but the most excessive care were his dusty English riding-boots. The unique combination of being a quiet, but determined roughneck who could handle himself almost professionally in a fistfight and an Ivy League graduate and scion of a distinguished Philadelphia family made Speck spectacularly popular. He became the undisputed leader of a group of young eastern college grads who added class, elegance, and excitement to the ever-growing mining community. They became known as the "Socialites."

· This hard-drinking, fun-loving group of men were all under thirty, all ambitious, all ready to party at the drop of a hat. Most were prosperously dressed, and the majority owned degrees from eastern colleges. By far the most attractive group of males in Cripple Creek, the Socialites attracted the camp's prettiest girls — professional and amateur alike — who gravitated toward them naturally. This gang kept the Crik's bars and dance halls roaring when everyone else collapsed from sheer exhaustion or the telling effects of high altitude and alcohol. The Socialites considered it open season on everything, and policemen existed only to see that the fighting was fair.

What set these future gold barons apart from the silver kings, railroad builders, and copper kings of Montana? The difference was vast! These men had been born wealthy, had expensive taste for rare wines, fine horses, evening attire, and polo.

Although not a college man, Tutt was accepted into the group. Devereux, a pleasant fellow when sober, but terror in his cups, and Leonard, the improbable westerner with a New York accent, were also members. Leonard, the slightly built Columbia grad who now worked as a miner, was Speck's roommate sharing bachelor quarters on Prospect Street atop the hill near the reservoir in the north part of town. Devereux, the former Princeton football star, was known lately for his skill on the polo fields.

Other Socialites included Henry Blackmer, a Boston blue blood, a lawyer, and sharpest of the crowd that Speck had met in Colorado Springs; Jimmie Burns, too good-looking and neat to be an itinerant miner, but naming that as his profession, who concentrated on having a good time; Verner Z. Reed, Chicago Tribune reporter, who had been a

The Penrose-Leonard cabin, built on the hillside above Cripple Creek, was the home of the two men shown here, Harry Leonard on the left and Speck. Leonard was also an Easterner who attended Columbia University in New York and a member of the Socialites. He worked as a stage coach driver before trying to make his fortune in gold. Speck and his white horse, Rabbit, were a familiar sight in the mining town.

Denver Public Library, #706

short-time resident of Colorado Springs while helping his father run a livery stable, and who was now becoming a slick real estate promoter; and Charlie MacNeill, a sharp-faced, brilliant young Chicago chemist, who was considered one of the best milling experts and hardest drinkers in the West. Continuing the list were Albert Eugene Carlton, from Warren, Illinois, the former TB victim Speck had met in Colorado Springs, and his brother Leslie, both grubstaked by their father with $10,000 with which they founded the Colorado Trading and Transfer Company, and "Big Bill" Haywood, a red-hot radical with an eye on politics.

By far the most spectacular was Gene Carlton, who suffered from ulcers and lost the use of one lung. This pale lad with the ice-blue eyes was still energetic enough to simultaneously handle a diversity of women in his life, including a wife in Illinois, a fiancee in Colorado Springs, a true love in Cripple Creek, and a pretty secretary name Ethel Frizell.

Speck himself had such poise and self-esteem that he evoked a haughty impression. But his bully-like personality and skill at fist fighting made him the unanimous choice to head this lively group of college men.

The Socialites established a plush, exclusive club off limits to women of even the highest social order, although their most popular rendezvous were the Myers Avenue parlor houses. When things became too lively and got out of hand, Speck stepped in and restored order. None of the Socialites challenged his authority after watching him beat up a few husky miners in street brawls. These fights usually ensued when someone, influenced by excessive potions of alcoholic beverage, would ridicule Speck's well known attire that included the riding-breeches, appropriate coat and vest, gloves and boots, and ever-present wide brimmed hat.

Penrose had been quick to use his fists in college and during his sojourn in Mexico, and seldom, if ever, did he come out second best. He had a powerful physique, but what his challengers did not know was that he had taken those boxing lessons at twenty-five cents apiece from an off-campus instructor while at Harvard. Had the institution accredited this course with appropriate credits, Speck would have graduated magna cum laude. To emphasize his scorn of those who were critical of his mode of attire, Speck ordered full-dress suits from the East, including white tie and tails, and often dressed for dinner.

None of the Socialites were ready for marriage, possibly because none had earned that first million. Speck had as a constant reminder his father's advice on how to escape the wiles of women, and he cautiously avoided becoming enamored by any attractive lady who displayed the slightest interest in marriage.

But he had one close call. One of the smart, pretty girls on the prowl for a husband was Sarah Elizabeth (Sally) Halthusen, a big-busted, dark-eyed brunette of Spanish-Swedish extraction whose hobby was breaking wild horses. A Denver father was rumored to have paid her $10,000 to break her engagement to his son. She had met Speck in Colorado Springs and lost no time in getting to the mining camp, living first on her father's ranch at nearby Florissant and, later, in a house on Bennett Avenue.

Speck appeared to have been captivated by her even after learning of the aforesaid ransom. Soon Cripple Creekers were gossiping about her repeated trips, astride her own white horse, to the Penrose-Leonard shack on Prospect Hill. The story persists that word of this romance reached the austere Dr. Penrose in Philadelphia who is said to have asked Dick, a frequent visitor to Cripple Creek in his profession capacity, to point out to Speck the impropriety of a Pennsylvania blue blood marrying a Colorado animal trainer. The white horse suddenly ceased the visits to the Prospect shack and Sally, convinced of her fruitless quest, returned to Colorado Springs and married Thomas Gough, a baker who owned the Chicago Bakery.

While enjoying the surge of real estate and mining brokerage prosperity, Tutt and Penrose had not overlooked that other purpose for which they were in Cripple Creek — development of the C.O.D. Mine. They had made some progress obtaining part of the money needed for development through the sale of shares. Speck had ear-marked one-third interest, but needed most of the money to pay for it. He invested the $150 Boies had sent him and whatever else he could scrape up. Speck prepared a glowing prospectus that was liberally circulated in Colorado Springs and Denver. Finally, through Speck's tireless ingenuity and sweat in Cripple Creek and Tutt's hard push in Colorado Springs real estate, they had the money needed for further development of the mine. It was decided late in July, 1893, that activities would officially begin at the C.O.D.

CHAPTER VIII

New Life
at the C.O.D.

It was July 21, 1893, the day before the official reopening of the C.O.D. Mine — a perfect time to reflect on
the bustling mountain community that would be the site of
this spectacular event. As the mid-summer sun disappeared
behind Mount Pisgah, west of town, there was a frenzy of
activity along Bennett Avenue, Cripple Creek's busiest thor-
oughfare. By 9 p.m. crowds loitered on the covered board-
walk in front of the Palace Hotel where the stage, drawn by
six horses, had just arrived from Florissant. East on Bennett
Avenue, the Gold Dollar Bar, the Turf, Saratoga, and Tom
Lorimer's Office Club filled up with patrons. Across the
avenue, below Second Street, Alonzo Welty's Stables was
turning business away. On down the street, busy with buggies, wagons, and horses, and bordered with electric poles,
James Bald's Market, N. O. Johnson's Department Store,
and Lampman's Undertaking Parlor closed up for the night,
though Lampman's might reopen if the occasion arose.

Store fronts, often with awnings, formed tall, wooden
facades decorated with crudely painted signs. At the Pueblo
House, Ducy's Exchange, and O. K. Shaving and Bath House,

customers ate, drank, and schemed for the next day. Almost twenty of these establishments crowded onto both sides of Bennett Avenue between Second and Third Streets.

Sounds of the boomtown all blended into a harmony of excitement. The aroma of mountain pine and cedar, stale beer, spilled whiskey, and horse manure couldn't be missed.

Further east on Bennett, Johnny Nolan's gambling house and saloon, next door to the Topic Dance Hall that featured a tin-horn band and taxi-dance girls, was the loudest and liveliest spot going. Through Nolan's swinging doors, the trade settled down to some serious drinking while being pursued, not too subtly, by prostitutes. The heavy, wooden, handcrafted bar had a metal foot rail, bordered by brass spittoons. A large framed mirror gave the room a bigger appearance. According to a popular legend, anyone who bellied up to the bar and demanded less than a gallon of rye and two fingers of water was considered a big sissy.

At the far end of Nolan's bar, a group of men were celebrating. They lifted their single-jack whiskey glasses in a toast "to the C.O.D.," the mine that had been dormant for many months, but would be reactivated tomorrow. Their attention focused on a spectacularly handsome, dapper, young man standing in their midst. It was Speck, part owner of the C.O.D. His face, fixed in a dead-pan glare, was unreadable but not expressionless, and one eyebrow seemed frozen in a sardonic high-cocked position.

Suddenly the group greeted a slim, red-whiskered man who entered the saloon carrying a carpet bag. It was Charles Tutt, partner of Penrose and major owner of the C.O.D., just in from his home in Colorado Springs for the reopening of the mine. Another ceremonious toast to the C.O.D. called for another round of drinks. That night, while leaning on the bar nursing their whiskey, the Socialites maintained their reputation for long, hard drinking.

To climax their evening the group got a surprise from giant Horace Devereux, usually a mild-mannered sort despite his size and athletic prowess. With each slug of whiskey, he slowly became a terror. Deep-rooted animalistic instincts rose to the surface.

Incensed by a miner's remark characterizing polo as a sport for weak, rich, and idle gentlemen, Devereux tossed the hulky miner from the bar squarely to the center of a poker table where a high-stakes game was in progress. Coins, cards, folding money, and players scattered over the room as the heavy miner hit the table with such a force that it collapsed and splintered into several pieces. It took the Socialites almost an hour to quell the disturbance and calm down their Princetonian.

One of the outstanding fetes of the Socialites was their ability, even after such a night of wild, hell-kicking revelry, to rise early the following day. Speck Penrose and Charles Tutt were no exception this July twenty-first evening. Tutt joined Penrose and Harry Leonard at their cabin north of town, and they managed to get a few hours sleep before the rays of the morning sun reached over Pikes Peak to signal the dawn of July twenty-second.

Partners, Penrose and Tutt planned a brief ceremony to officially reactivate their C.O.D. Mine. From their cabin high on the hillside, Speck, astride his beautiful white horse, Rabbit, and Tutt, on his fine black mare, set out for the mine. Harry Leonard washed up and shaved, readying himself for his part-time job as a Cheyenne Mountain Stage driver.

Coming down the hill, just below the reservoir where the Penrose-Leonard cabin perched, the panoramic view was invigorating, particularly at this hour of the morning. The inhabitants were rising from the unpainted shacks huddled tightly together in the central pocket of the little town. Miners trudged on foot to their work. Straight ahead stood the inspiring sight of the Sangre de Cristo mountains and the Continental Divide. Tutt and Speck rode down Third Street, over on Eaton Avenue to Fourth, then down Carr Avenue and on east of town to Poverty Gulch. This area sat at the lower part of Pikes Peak. The mine was across the gulch from the Womack discovery, first in the district.

The opening ceremony consisted primarily of having their picture taken beside their respective mounts in front of the crude shaft. Speck appeared disdainfully proud and self-assured. His smile was forced since he seldom smiled. Underneath, however, he may not have been so confident. One wonders if he was thinking of his father who so seldom approved of what he did. Perhaps he would at last be proud of his son as the new part-owner of a gold mine. Could this finally be the turning point of Speck's life? As he looked into the camera, Speck could see beyond the lens, back to the long, hard disappointing struggle that began almost twenty-eight years before in the City of Brotherly Love.

CHAPTER IX

ALL THAT
GLITTERS IS GOLD

So it was on July 22, 1893, as the camera documented the grand opening of the C.O.D., Speck reflected on the rough and tumble road that had led him to this point in his life. Finally Speck was established. Perhaps not as his father, Dr. Penrose, would have liked, but nevertheless, Speck had found his niche in life in the Rockies of Colorado's gold country.

By now humanity was pouring into Cripple Creek in almost a steady stream of wagon loads. Many who were broke, walked. They came from every direction — miners and their families looking for work, union organizers, dreamers, lawyers, prospectors, claim jumpers, saloon keepers, laborers, salesmen, prostitutes and their madams, drifters, financiers, railroad men, and aristocrats from Colorado Springs, Boston, Philadelphia, London, and elsewhere — all with an inordinate lust for gold.

Most of the new residents of Cripple Creek who had heard his story wanted to emulate the man everyone was talking about...Winfield Scott Stratton. Twenty-seven-year-old Speck was no different from the rest.

Stratton was a former three-dollar-a-day carpenter from Colorado Springs who spent his summers prospecting for precious metals in the district long before the gold boom and prior to the time the camp was given its name. He was born in Jeffersonville, Indiana, in 1848, which made him forty-three years old at the time of his first big discovery at the Independence — the first big Cripple Creek gold strike on a date documented by western historians as July 4, 1891. Because of his rugged life, Stratton seemed much older, particularly to the young Socialites. At the time of Stratton's birth, General Winfield "Fuss and Feathers" Scott, Chief-of-Staff of the U.S. Army, was riding the crest of his Mexican War popularity. Myron Stratton, who sired twelve children, eight of them girls, gave his son the name of his war hero, as did many others throughout the country.

Winfield Scott was the only son who survived. In his late teens, he left home because he got tired of being surrounded by his eight sisters. He headed west, working as a carpenter in Nebraska before coming to Colorado Springs in 1872. He set up a shop on Pikes Peak Avenue and soon prospered as a good carpenter who possessed a mathematical mind that helped him make unerring estimates.

In 1876, at the age of twenty-eight, and after four months of courtship, he married Zeurah V. Stewart, a seventeen-year-old Illinois girl. Neighbors said they quarreled incessantly, probably because of Stratton's explosive temper. When Zeurah told him that she was pregnant, he flew into a rage, and after a short time, he took her back to Danville, Illinois, leaving her penniless. He divorced her three years later.

Stratton was a serious, highly tempered, and impulsive sort whose sober countenance suggested that he had never enjoyed a good laugh in his life. He sunk $2,800 of his

Pikes Peak Library District
Special Collections

Winfield Scott Stratton, one of the early arrivals in Cripple Creek, staked his claim at the Independence Mine and stayed with it until gold appeared. He left the area before the Socialites really began to show up, but some of the more astute, such as Tutt and Penrose, relied on him for advice. He was seldom wrong. Early in the gold boom, Verner Z. Reed sold Stratton's Independence Mine for eleven million dollars.

Courtesy, Pikes Peak Library District.

carpentry earnings in the Yretaba silver lode in the San Juan Mountains. He was one of the first to locate claims in the Cripple Creek District, having had the counsel of Bob Womack, the Kentucky-born cowboy first to discover gold there in 1891. After Stratton's first big strike, the mountain area overnight became known as "The Largest Gold Camp on Earth," with the population exploding from that moment on. As Stratton's success mounted, the story of his life quickly became an open book.

For the run-of-the-mill miner in Cripple Creek, success was hard to come by. If the original discovery with its superficial deposits did not get bought out by the big money boys from San Francisco or the East, incompetence, gambling, drink, and lead poisoning robbed them of their small holdings. They would be forced out eventually anyway because it took money and machinery to go deeper into the hard rock.

After activities commenced at the C.O.D., Speck and Tutt were both shrewd enough to be genuinely interested in the economic advancement of their community. Before Tutt returned to Colorado Springs, the partners decided to investigate the possibilities of still another venture. They saw the need of a sampling works in Cripple Creek. Their sampler would be a processing plant where ore could be bought from small mine owners at a price per ton, determined by assay samples.

For support of this scheme they resolved to appeal to Winfield Stratton, who had become one of the first gold millionaires from the Crik. Although now a resident of Colorado Springs, he happened to be in Cripple Creek tending to new developments in his Independence Mine. Stratton was a logical choice. His foremost interest was always in the small operators and the working class. He knew that many owners of undeveloped mines could not afford to ship their ore to a smelter or a mill and that a local sampler would be a great help to them. So the partners approached Stratton with their plan.

Although Stratton had exhibited a tendency toward impulsiveness in his private life, when it came to business he was as rational as a court judge. He saw real merit in this idea and told the young men that he would support it. Before he could change his mind, the Tutt-Penrose team set out for Colorado Springs to raise the money necessary for their plan. With Stratton's endorsement of the proposed sampling deal, Colorado Springs bankers advanced the money without hesitation. As a result of this financial backing the partners organized the Cripple Creek Sampling & Ore Company and quickly drew up plans to build a plant.

Now Tutt and Penrose had a wider array of business operations than anyone else in the Crik. They were brokers in real estate and mining shares, mine operators, and the latest development put them into gold ore processing. Since Speck was on the scene in the mining camp, it was necessary for him to assume the majority of the responsibility. For most, it would have been an awesome task, but the twenty-seven-year-old entrepreneur thrived on the day-to-day pressure of this growing enterprise.

While Speck worked hard, he played hard too. As the leader of the Socialites he felt obligated to set the pace for the rowdy crowd. As a result, he was constantly on the move. Speck was beginning to make history in mining circles and in the kerosene hot spots of the day-or-night. His horse Rabbit could be found nightly, hitched at the tie rail in front of the Ironside Dancery or Johnny Nolan's place or the Topic Dance Hall. Rabbit cultivated a taste for lump sugar soaked in gin.

Among the property owned by Tutt and Penrose Real Estate Company was the two-story Topic Dance Hall where afternoon and evening taxi-dances were held in addition to a variety of other activities. These spots were popularly referred to as "Speculatoriums." The traffic in prostitution was heavy there, but it was one block south on Myers Avenue where most of the good times and trouble originated. In the one-woman cribs, customers had a wide choice of women. In the first row of cribs were the French prostitutes; next the Spanish; then Oriental; and finally Negro. There was a generous sprinkling of just plain white professional sinners as well.

Many of the madams were gaining national notoriety as well as fortunes. There was Pearl deVere, and Cock-eyed Liz, and the scarlet atmosphere that abided at the Old Homestead which made it the most elegant bordello in town. There was also Portia of the Tenderloin, a female attorney who defended in court many of the denizens of Myers Avenue, including French Blanche, who had a baby and wanted to take care of it. The girls didn't mind, but the good women of Cripple Creek did.

In addition to patronizing the Myers Avenue bordellos, the miners drank heavily, gambled, and occasionally killed. However most of these activities took money, and the regular miners were earning only three dollars for a nine-hour day. This widened the already cavernous gap between the mine owners and the miners. It also marked the beginning of rumblings from the miners for more pay. To gain collective strength, the miners were rapidly affiliating with the Western Federation of Miners, headquartered in Denver where fiery Big Bill Haywood, a Socialite from Cripple Creek, was executive secretary. This conflict between the two principal

In March of 1894, partners Tutt (far right) and Penrose (second from the left) stand in front of their Cripple Creek office with two business associates. By this time the real estate business had grown to include a mine, mining stock, and ownership and operation of the Cripple Creek Sampling and Ore Company. Courtesy, Pikes Peak Library District.

elements of Cripple Creek created an atmosphere of tension, some said to be the reason Speck Penrose never smiled.

Added to the growing unrest of the miners, Tutt and Penrose had their hands full. They were struggling to put their Sampling and Ore Company into full operation, striving to keep their real estate and mining shares business going at the previously-set accelerated rate, and there was now trouble at their C.O.D. Mine. One day the mine filled up with water, so in desperation Speck wired his geologist brother Dick for advice. Dick Penrose had co-authored a standard reference on the area, *Geology & Mining Industries of the Cripple Creek District*. He recommended pumping out the C.O.D., a practice that was common in the district. The biggest difficulty was the lack of capital to get the pumps going. Their financial resources had dwindled as other businesses started to slip as well.

The partners decided to adopt a plan that would provide them some cash and at the same time keep activity going at the C.O.D. They would lease the mine. There were two men in the area interested, so Tutt and Penrose drew up the papers and leased the mine for $20,000.

The lease holders, Joe Troy and Pete Burke, sank a new shaft and hit squarely on the apex of one of the best defined veins in the district. It was a great new strike! The C.O.D. became a producer and, under the terms of the lease, Tutt and Penrose shared in the profits. Now there was truly reason for celebration and revelry. The Socialites went all out for their leader who had worked so hard for this moment. Speck's ship had finally come in. They had the greatest gold-strike party in Cripple Creek's history. No one stayed sober. None arose early the next day because they were still going full blast. And Speck smiled uninhibitedly throughout the night!

By the end of the year 1893, the disastrous effects of the nationwide panic became more and more intensified, particularly in the minds of Troy and Burke. The full collapse of silver mining in Colorado was another hard fact to swallow for the lease holders of the C.O.D. They prevailed on Tutt and Penrose to buy back the lease. Speck and Charles felt, that since they had everything they owned tied up in the success or failure of the gold mining industry in Cripple Creek, they had little more to lose by taking back the C.O.D., especially in light of the new vein that had been uncovered. Although they were short of cash and outside money for Colorado mining investments was tight, the resourceful team managed to buy back the C.O.D. lease. Penrose had the ability to attract capital where no one else could.

Despite the shaky conditions of the nation's economy, Penrose and Tutt were bordering on a success. Speck Penrose had turned twenty-eight years old and his partner was only a year older. Back in Philadelphia, Speck's father heard about these latest developments and could not believe it. Speck could not possibly succeed at the remote gold mining community in the Rocky Mountains. Dr. Penrose was seldom wrong.

CHAPTER X

THE BATTLE OF BULL HILL

B esides Speck and his partner, other members of the Socialites were also making good in their endeavors. The Carltons had made a success of the Colorado Trading and Transfer Company; Henry Blackmer had been elected El Paso County Attorney in 1892 and was now aiming for the District Attorney's job; Verner Reed now resided at the Palace Hotel where he loved the gilded living and the great ease and ability he possessed to earn money by selling mining property.

Reed found that there was great interest in Colorado mining property abroad, so he moved his operation to Europe. While waiting there for bigger things to happen, he sold the C.O.D. to a French syndicate for $300,000, of which Tutt and Penrose got $240,000 after Reed raked off his commission. The Frenchmen deepened the shaft and eventually went broke trying to unwater the C.O.D. — another stroke of luck for the partners.

Shortly after banking his share of the profit from the sale of the mine, Speck made a trip to Philadelphia to visit his father and brothers. His brother, State Senator Boies

Penrose and a candidate for mayor of the City of Brotherly Love, was in a bitter campaign. Speck knew that this was an expensive venture, so he brought along $10,000 in gold which he plunked down on Boies' desk.

"What's that?" inquired the Senator.

"Your share of the grubstake," replied Speck.

"But I didn't send you the $10,000 you asked for," returned Boies. "I wired you $150 for expenses home."

"So," added Speck, "I invested the $150 and this is your share of the profit on the investment."

Back in Cripple Creek, Speck and Tutt became involved in a controversy that, sooner or later, besets virtually all mine owners — a labor dispute.

In 1892, Colorado voters, dissatisfied with both Republican and Democratic attitudes on labor and economic questions, had elected a Populist governor. He was Davis H. Waite, a sixty-seven-year-old resident of the silver mining community of Aspen whose only prerequisite was that he had been a justice of the peace. He horrified conservatives when he stated in a speech: "And if the money power shall attempt to sustain its usurpations by the strong hand, we shall meet the issue when it is forced upon us, for it is better, infinitely better, that blood should flow to the horses' bridles rather than our national liberties should be destroyed." This gained His Excellency the sobriquet of "Bloody Bridles."

While the Bloody Bridles speech shocked the mine owners of El Paso County, it delighted the miners, who were now confident that in the event of a showdown they could depend on the support of the governor. Bitterness was rapidly developing on both sides.

The owners' antagonists were Governor Waite, Populism, and Cripple Creek's Irish Catholic miners. The mine owners of Colorado Springs were principally Episcopalians who thought that the miners should be happy to accept the depressed wage scales prevailing throughout the country. The miners felt that they had as much right as the owners to benefit from Cripple Creek's booming prosperity.

The life of the miner was lonely, dangerous, and insecure. Few were fortunate enough to have wives to prepare their meals and boil their laundry. Most were forced to "batch it" or take up residence in a boarding house. Miners toiled nine hours a day with pick and shovel for only three dollars in wages. Blast holes for explosives were hand-drilled into the rock. Ore was hauled in wheelbarrows or small mine cars. The large mines hauled it out in tandem-hitched wagons drawn by many teams of horses or mules — over the dangerous mountain roads. Some mines used pack burros to transport ore. When a miner got hurt, his friends fed him until he could return to work. If he was killed in an accident, they passed the hat to bury him or to buy his wife and children transportation to their nearest kinfolk. When "pay dirt" petered out, as it often did, they had to seek jobs elsewhere.

John Calderwood, a Scotsman and former Aspen miner and therefore a friend of Governor Waite, had become an effective and sensible leader of the fast growing mine union. He had the respect and confidence of the owners as well as the miners. Early in April 1894, he went on a speaking tour for the federation. When he returned, all hell had broken loose. What was to have been a strike became the "Battle of Bull Hill."

Looking back on the Spring of 1894, Dick Penrose wrote that these were exciting days in Cripple Creek, for labor trouble between mine owners and mine workers resulted in them blowing up one mine and the death of several persons. And the state militia was called out.

During the strike, mine owners helped Sheriff Bowers recruit an army of deputies. Speck and Dick, who was in the area at the time, gathered up a group of dandies from the El Paso Club of Colorado Springs and formed Company K of the sheriff's army. Although they were engaged in the dead serious business of defending life and property, there was a ludicrous side to their mission.

Speck's constant concern, in contemplating his own welfare, was that he should always be near a sufficient supply of liquor. He became apprehensive that his comrades of Company K might not have enough to sustain them during the campaign. One night he took off on horseback for Colorado Springs where he found that drug stores had exhausted their whiskey stocks, but a Cascade Avenue mine owner donated a barrel of bourbon. He could hardly carry a barrel from the saddle so, inspired by the emergency, he stopped by Glockner Hospital where he bought a dozen rubber hot water bottles. He filled them with bourbon, strapped them to the saddle and returned triumphantly to Company K via the Cheyenne Mountain Road.

The strike resulted in vast destruction of property and many lives lost. The state militia and various groups of civilian deputies took part in the skirmishes. When a "treaty of peace" was signed June 10, 1894, the strike had lasted 130 days, the longest and most bitter of all U.S. labor disputes up to that time. The cost exceeded $3,000,000 in lost production, lost wages, property destruction, and the upkeep of the armies that had participated.

The miners won their demand for a three dollar, eight-hour day. Peace brought more prospectors, miners, and general populous. On July 1, 1894, the first Florissant and Cripple Creek passenger train arrived at the camp.

CHAPTER XI

A FORTUITOUS
TRAGEDY

As the gold camps grew, so grew the need for all forms of relaxation. In addition to the crowded saloons and popular tenderloin districts, outdoor sports were also pursued. In Gillett, for instance, a race track drew fans from the entire area. And early in 1895, the Gillett Bull Ring was built inside the oval of the race track with a seating capacity of 5,000 (Gillett itself had barely 1,000 at the time). On August 24, the nation's only bull fight was to be staged there. However, due to protests from certain Puritanical quarters, the show did not go on. Henry Blackmer became prosecutor in the Gillett Bull Fight Case.

In December of 1895, while thirty-one-year-old Tutt and thirty-year-old Penrose were wondering what to do with the profits from the sale of their C.O.D. Mine, Charlie MacNeill's Pioneer Reduction Mill was totally destroyed by fire. This would normally be a tragedy for MacNeill, but it turned out to be a fortuitous accident of fate for Tutt, Penrose, and MacNeill.

By the time he was twenty-one, MacNeill knew more about milling metal than most of the experts. He came to

Denver at fourteen when his father, Dr. J.E. MacNeill, moved from Chicago and worked as a protégé of mill expert Ed Holden. During the silver boom, Charlie MacNeill worked in smelters at Aspen, Leadville, and Denver. The brilliant young chemist arrived on the stage in Cripple Creek in 1893. As one of the original Socialites, he became a close friend with Speck and Tutt. Once he stole Jimmie Burn's current girl for no better reason than to win a bet from Speck. He got an experimental chlorination plant working in 1894, and did a big milling business. But it came to a halt in late 1895 when the mill burned to the ground.

MacNeill, Speck, and Tutt all considered themselves experienced mining men. They listened to their friend Bert Carlton who reasoned that the surest way to make money — big money— in a gold camp would be to corner its transportation and facilities for refining ore. Such a monopoly would leave its bosses free to charge whatever the traffic would bear. By this time, Bert had done just that and was starting to amass a fortune through his ore wagon transportation facilities.

Another friend who was enjoying a continued growth in prosperity was Stratton. Now in his forties he was respected for the honesty of his opinion and judgment; but he had one enemy — liquor, and one fear — matrimonial minded women. Many a widow and spinster in the Colorado Springs and Cripple Creek area yearned for a marriage proposal from him. But he was dead set on a minimum of woman trouble and doggedly stuck to his determination to stay single. He and his friends were patrons of the tenderloin on Myers Avenue in Cripple Creek and in Victor. When it occurred to them that it was undignified for men of their standing in the business community to be callers in the bedrooms of the parlor houses or the cribs, they instead had the girls call at regular intervals at their Battle Mountain shacks above Victor.

In 1895, one of Stratton's girls, Candy Root, sued him for $200,000 "heart balm," alleging, one, that he reneged on a promise to marry her and, two, that he was the father of her soon to be born child. He told the court that never had he proposed marriage to her, nor did he intend to marry her or any other girl, respectable or professional; and, that inasmuch as she had been busily practicing her profession for at least three years, how did she know who got her pregnant. Both counts were dismissed.

After discussing their plans in detail with men like Carlton and Stratton — Tutt, Penrose, and MacNeill pooled their resources and formed the Colorado-Philadelphia Reduction Company early in 1896. Joining this triumvirate were Speck's brother, Dick, and Wendall P. Bowman, who both became members of the board. Tutt was president, MacNeill, vice-president, and Speck, secretary-treasurer. They located their mill — not in Cripple Creek, but in Colorado City — on the northwest environs of Colorado Springs, forty miles from the gold camps. Over this scenic route they built the famous narrow-guage railroad, the Cripple Creek Short Line, to help bring ore to their mill. While this was going on, the real estate firm of Tutt and Penrose had earned nearly $200,000.

In March of 1896, both Speck and MacNeill moved to Colorado Springs where they could be closer to the big chlorination plant that milled most of Cripple Creek's output. With their mill, Tutt, Penrose, and MacNeill had a substantial start in becoming millionaires. So, at the age of thirty-one, Speck, the only bachelor of the trio, drew considerable interest from more than a score of eligible young ladies when he returned to Colorado Springs.

About one month after Speck took up residence in Colorado Springs, one of Cripple Creek's first great fires swept the mining camp. One might say that he got out in the nick of time, but the truth of the matter was that much of the property that he and Tutt owned was totally destroyed by the fire, including the Topic Dance Hall where afternoon taxi-dances would cease forever. If their property was not consumed by the first fire on April 25, 1896, most of it was leveled, along with the rest of Cripple Creek, in the second great fire just five days later. The wooden frame buildings and shacks simply burned to the ground, leaving nothing but rubble and almost 5,000 homeless.

While all of this was taking place in the Colorado Rockies, Boies Penrose was seeking a seat in the U.S. Senate. In January 1897, he was elected as the junior Republican from the state of Pennsylvania — the fulfillment of a long-desired political dream.

By this time, wealthy, good-looking Verner Reed was also a resident of Colorado Springs, where he was compared to F. Scott Fitzgerald as he quickly gained the reputation as a writer. He also got into the real estate promotion business in Colorado Springs and did so well that Winfield Stratton hired him to handle the messed up real estate operation of his Portland Mine, which Reed did straighten out.

At this point, as mentioned earlier, Reed started tiring of the West and decided to open up offices in London and Scotland to sell Cripple Creek mining stock. This is where he found the French syndicate that bought Tutt and Penrose's C.O.D. Mine. Afterwards he also swung a deal with the Venture Corporation of London for the sale of Stratton's Independence Mine for the amount of eleven million dollars — taking

Verner Z. Reed, a Chicago Tribune *reporter, lived a short time in Colorado Springs then came to Cripple Creek to join the excitement. There, he was a member of the Socialites and became a "slick" real estate promoter. Reed moved abroad to capitalize on the excellent market there for Rocky Mountain gold mines. Among other Cripple Creek mines, he sold the C.O.D., owned by his friends Tutt and Penrose.*

Denver Public Library Western Collection. F42644.

one million dollars himself as a commission for the sale. So, Reed was a millionaire at age thirty-six.

After six years of prosperity, the sale of the Independence made Stratton one of the wealthiest men in the area. He became one of the most publicized mining men of the country — and the world. He made all of his vast wealth in gold after the collapse of the silver industry. His compassion for the working class turned his sympathies in their direction. Of several public utterances, his most notable occurred during the 1896 presidential campaign between the ultra-conservative gold bug, William McKinley, the Republican, and William Jennings Bryan, the Democratic champion of bimetalism. During the heat of the campaign, Stratton offered to bet $100,000 that Bryan would win. This drew nation-wide attention when there were no takers. The Republicans alternately suffered chills and fever in the fear that this presaged defeat for McKinley who eventually won by half a million votes. Cripple Creek, the greatest gold camp in the nation, gave Bryan 3,000 votes to 700 for McKinley. Bryan carried Colorado by 130,000.

The same antagonists faced each other in the 1900 presidential election. Stratton was now richer by far than he was in 1896, having sold his Independence Mine in 1899, but remained unwavering in his loyalty to Bryan and the cause of silver. He again posted a bet of $100,000 that Bryan would win. This time he found a taker. His name was Spencer Penrose. That was the first big political bet that Speck won.

Another great fire destroyed the town of Victor in August of 1899. But the industrious miners moved quickly to rebuild it just as they did Cripple Creek after its two devastating fires. By 1900, there were 150 saloons in the district, seventy-five in Cripple Creek alone. The camps and their saloons, "sin streets," and mining activity were still booming, so much so, that Theodore Roosevelt, on his 1901 presidential campaign trail, visited Cripple Creek and stayed at the home of J. Maurice Finn, an attorney and acquaintance of Speck's.

In Colorado Springs, Tutt, Penrose, and MacNeill became directors at the Colorado Title & Trust Company, which was organized in 1901. Other directors included Bert Carlton, William Slocum, and C.C. Hamlin. This was Speck's only bank connection.

The partners, Tutt, MacNeill, and Penrose itched for a complete monopoly in gold milling. By 1901, under Penrose's leadership, they formed the United States Reduction and Refining Company and went to New York to arrange for $13,000,000 to launch the project.

As Dr. Penrose said in his letter to Dick:

> ...Spencer and partners have concluded their deal, $13,000,000. It all sounds very fine. Tutt and MacNeill had gone back to Colorado. Spencer in the meantime is making the Atlantic his headquarters and going to New York when required. He expects to be East some two weeks longer. But both he and Tutt expect to be constantly East as they were to have an office in New York.

Dick was also caught up in the enthusiasm. Though, less sarcastic and cynical, he wrote:

> I have also received a letter from Speck about the mill consolidation. I think the scheme is most excellent and Speck, Tutt, and MacNeill deserve the greatest credit for the way they have carried the deal through.

Again Dr. Penrose writes:

>...Spencer doubtless has posted you on what they all think a very desirable deal — certainly on paper, it looks very fine and gives us all on paper a great increase in our holdings.

Never, did Dr. Penrose ever indicate even the slightest signs of confidence in his son, Spencer. This is obvious by the letters he wrote and by the conversations he held with friends and relatives, alike.

Speck and his two partners spent much of their time on the east coast raising money, signing bonds, negotiating with bankers and investors, and meeting with attorneys. Naturally, Speck took advantage of this opportunity to see his father and brothers in Philadelphia.

Speck had made his residence in Cripple Creek for five years. He had come down from the mountain a millionaire and entered the swim of Little London's social whirl. Although he was active at the Cheyenne Mountain Country Club, where he had created such a spectacular scene only ten years earlier, he favored the El Paso Club that was walking distance from his office. It had been organized on May 7, 1878, at a meeting of business and professional men in the Gayette Building.

On January 11, 1901, Speck and a bachelor friend, Clarence Edsall, hosted a "clambake" at the El Paso Club to which thirty guests were invited. Among them was a pretty, blue-eyed, warmly responsive blonde, Julie Villiers Lewis McMillan (Mrs. James H. McMillan), who had brought her husband to Colorado Springs in the hope of curing the tuberculosis (they called consumption) he had contracted in Cuba during the Spanish American War. He died a few months later. Penrose barely noticed his lovely guest.

Life as a bachelor, and a rich one at that, in Colorado Springs agreed with Speck. There were plenty of parties and, in addition to Tutt, Speck now had many friends living in Colorado Springs. He was still ill at ease and awkward with the socially prominent north-end girls, which can best be illustrated by a sample of his attempts at social chit-chat, "Do you or don't you" he would ask, "...play tennis?"

Activities at the El Paso Club alone would have been enough to keep most men busy. By this time, Speck had developed an even greater taste and capacity for whiskey, women, and the finer things in life, although he was constantly preoccupied with the mill trust, money-raising trips to the East, and other businesses still booming in the Crik despite the fires. In 1899, thirty-four-year-old Speck took a trip around the world. And the next year, he vacationed in Cuba with his brother Tal.

On June 8, 1901, Speck's youngest brother, Phillip, at the age of thirty-two, died suddenly while on a trip to El Paso, Texas. Now there were only five Penrose brothers — Boies, Tal, Speck, Dick and Francis. And "Friday," or Francis, had been a hopeless invalid since he contracted "brain fever" six years before.

Partly in an attempt to introduce Boies and Tal to his western country, and partly to find some relaxation and diversion from the tension that had built up during the money-raising program and the sudden death of his brother, Speck arranged to have a hunting expedition for Tal, Boies, and Dick in Ketchum, Idaho. On August 15, 1901, the brothers met in Gardiner, Montana, then proceeded to Ketchum. The result was several elk trophies and everyone benefiting from the outdoor experience. As Dr. Penrose said in a letter to Dick, who at the last minute could not make the trip:

> Spencer writes in good spirits from Colorado Springs. Indeed, the hunting trip seems to have benefited the crowd vastly, and Boies and Tal never looked better, and Tal says Spencer is equally fine.

While the rest of this nation's attention was on the McKinley assassination in 1901, thirty-five-year-old Speck and his partners blanketed the Cripple Creek Mining District with mills built with the money they raised for the new U.S. Reduction and Refining Company. They now had a complete monopoly for milling the gold from "The Largest Gold Camp on Earth." The mill trust was despised and castigated and bitterly fought on both sides of Pikes Peak because of the high prices squeezed out of mine owners. At the same time, Speck's friends, Carlton and Blackmer, had a transportation monopoly.

Early in 1902, Cripple Creek's population had exploded at such a rate that the Jack Johnson — "Mexican Pete" prize fight was staged there. The nation's attention focused on the grueling twenty rounds that Johnson finally won.

Shortly afterwards in Colorado Springs, William Stratton died at the prime of his success. He was only fifty-four. After his death, thirteen women, each one claiming to have been secretly married to him, sued for a share of his vast estate.

CHAPTER XII

THE COPPER KING

By early 1902 everything business wise was going at an extraordinary pace for thirty-six-year-old Speck. There was the profit from the sale of the C.O.D., the real estate business was at an all-time high, and the mill trust was far better than a score of gold mines because that venture was much less risky and everyone who made a strike contributed a substantial profit to the owners.

Dr. Penrose had still only taken a very small part in any of Speck's deals. He was reluctant to do so even with Dick's assurance that it was all right. He was dubious about Spencer's activities as indicated in a letter written on January 20, 1902, to Dick while he was abroad in Venice, Italy.

> Spencer is here, is a good deal in New York in connection with his mill business, seems to be having a good time and also seems to be well satisfied with the condition of his affairs. I don't pretend to understand half, but will bide my time until you return to explain it all to me.

The mill trust hired a brilliant metallurgist from Missouri, Daniel Cowan Jackling, for their mill at Colorado City.

Jackling's story is as romantic as that of any Horatio Alger yarn — a poor farm boy who worked his way through the Missouri School of Mines and walked to Cripple Creek in its early boom days from a railroad station twenty miles away because he did not have the fare necessary to ride the stage that connected Cripple Creek to Divide.

Jackling had worked for MacNeill in Cripple Creek some years before. He had left for Utah where he experimented with a vast deposit of low grade copper ore at Bingham Canyon. He had an obsession about the Utah property, believing that with a new type of copper mill he could refine the two percent Bingham Canyon ore and make it profitabile. By 1900, the high grade copper ore (five to twenty-five percent) was dwindling rapidly and the demand for copper was increasing with the dawn of the Electrical Age.

In 1903, Bingham was just another mining community near Salt Lake City. It was one of the oldest of the Utah mining districts, having been worked since 1864, with its early history centered on production of salacious gold ore and silver-bearing lead ores.

Jackling first discussed his plan with MacNeill, who displayed some interest; but it was Speck Penrose who began to show the greater interest. Speck had an ace in the hole in the person of his brother Dick, by this time an eminent geologist and mining consultant. Dick thought Jackling's plan workable.

So on June 1, 1903, MacNeill, Speck, and Dick accompanied Jackling to Salt Lake City, then rode to the mine by horse and wagon. At the last minute it was decided that a young lawyer by the name of C.C. Hamlin — recently a member of the Wyoming legislature — would join the group to make things legal. It was a twelve mile trek from Salt Lake

City to Bingham Canyon. After tramping over the ground for a while, they held an informal conference on the hillside and eventually moved their discussion to Salt Lake City and the veranda of the Knutsford Hotel. There, enthusiasm for Jackling's scheme seemed to increase with each round of drinks. Since Dick Penrose was in favor of the project, the matter was settled. That evening, at a cost of $100, Jackling gave a dinner at the hotel to commemorate the occasion.

On June 4, 1903, the Utah Copper Company was incorporated for $500,000 in one-dollar shares. This money was needed to build the proposed pilot plant. MacNeill and Penrose, as bankers and promoters, took 250,000 shares. MacNeill needled Speck into pledging the $100,000 he had won from the late multimillionaire W.S. Stratton on McKinley's election bet.

On June 15, 1903, Dick wrote this letter to his father from Salt Lake City describing the launching of their company:

> I wrote you last from Colorado Springs. From there Speck, MacNeill, Tutt, and I came here, where we have been working for the past few days perfecting the details of our copper deal. We have organized a company called the Utah Copper Company and will carry on our operations in this way instead of as individuals. Speck and MacNeill wanted me to be president of the company, but I did not accept, as I did not want to be tied down too much, and I can be just as much use to the company without being an officer, so they elected me a director. They elected MacNeill president, and Speck secretary and treasurer, and an excellent man named Jackling, general manager. Tutt will probably be vice-president.

We are gradually getting in shape here to go to work, and by the time we leave we hope to have made satisfactory preliminary arrangements. Our idea is to erect as soon as possible a mill with a capacity of about 500 tons of ore daily. It will take several months to finish this, and MacNeill and Jackling will look after the construction while Speck is on his hunting trip and I am in Alaska.

We have spent a lot of time in making arrangements with the principal owner of the copper mine for the interests that we have options on from him, but this matter is now settled, and the papers are in the bank ready to be taken up by us if, after our mill is built, we decide that it is wise to put up the remaining money due on the property.

We are today trying to get a suitable place to locate the mill, and as we need a lot of water for the mill, it is necessary to be very careful in the selection of location, but we hope to get one.

Speck and MacNeill return to Colorado Springs tomorrow, and from there Speck goes to join Boies in British Columbia....

They decided to secure control of Bingham Canyon, which had been turned down by the top men and firms in the industry, so Speck, MacNeill, and Tutt each pledged $100,000 of the half-million. The mill trust took 50,000 shares, and the balance was subscribed by Speck's family — finally Dr. Penrose succumbed and was joined by his successful sons Boies and Tal who by now felt that their ne'er-do-well brother, Speck, somehow possessed a Midas touch. Naturally, Dick led the way since it was his prognostication that set them off. Only his endorsement of the project induced the Penrose family members to invest in this wholly new and untried business. Dr. Penrose still did not have full confidence in Speck despite his son's successes. Later Dr. Penrose's misgivings were proven wrong.

Jackling's innovative approach showed that low-grade ore could be mined from the surface by use of steam shovels. New methods of extracting the metal from the ore were being devised which resulted in a high grade concentrate for smelting. With their success, the group bought three gold mines: the Granite, the Gold Coin, and the Ajax.

However, there were months of torment during the period that Jackling's mill was under construction because labor troubles at the mills in Cripple Creek District had reduced the income of the three members of the trust. They could have been completely wiped out overnight by the failure of Jackling's process.

In 1902, the people of Colorado approved a constitutional amendment commanding the legislature to enact an eight-hour-day law, but when the assembly convened in 1903 no action was taken.

The Western Federation of Miners called a strike at the Colorado Reduction and Refining Company at Colorado City, demanding wage increases and the eight-hour-day. Nine union men involved were fired.

Haywood decided on a show of power. He called a strike of miners in Cripple Creek to paralyze the flow of ore to the Colorado City reduction plant. Some 3,500 miners from fifty mines answered the call.

The mine owners replied by bringing in miners who were watched over by armed guards, but union agitators spurred the miners on to even more demands from the wealthy mine owners. The tension became so great that on the third of

September the militia was called out again to maintain the peace. This time the battle between employer and employee lasted far longer than 130 days. It continued for almost one year. Speck became a member of the staff of Governor James H. Peabody, with the rank of colonel. The bloodiest force met force. Men battled for their jobs. Strikers and strikebreakers were killed in open battle on the hills above Cripple Creek and Victor. Dynamite ripped down shaft houses and twisted bridges. Hundreds of miners were herded into trains that crossed the Kansas and New Mexico state lines with orders never to return, reinforced with buckshot. The newspapers referred to it as the "Cripple Creek Labor War." The war came to a climax on June 6, 1904, when the Independence station in Cripple Creek was blown up, resulting in thirteen dead and fourteen injured.

Although he was unaware of it at the time, Charlie Mac-Neill was being stalked by Harry Orchard, one of the most despicable and dangerous characters in the country. His purpose was to murder MacNeill who was considered an "arch enemy of the strikers." Although he was unsuccessful in his attempts because of circumstances that came out later in his trial, Orchard did succeed in killing many others and destroying mining property with his prime weapon, a bomb.

President Theodore Roosevelt finally recalled the national guard on July 26, 1904, thus ending the longest and most bloody labor dispute in history up to that time.

In the meantime, Speck's copper mining, gold milling and real estate operation was steadily expanding. On December 5, 1905, Tutt announced to his partners and the world that he was retiring from the mountain activities and confining himself from then on to real estate in Colorado Springs. This he did, but later the mining magnate ventured out to the west coast where he became known as an international yachtsman. He, his relatives and friends sailed the Pacific on his ocean-going sailing vessel, the "Anemone." Tutt's retirement left Speck and MacNeill, known as Cripple Creek's most accomplished single-jack drinkers, a larger share of the operation and ultimately more profits.

Utah Copper stock bounced around the market at a low price. Tutt sold his stock in Utah Copper for what he had paid, $100,000. He felt that he had pressed his luck far enough and he was interested in mining property in Oregon. Speck bought Tutt's stock on the open market.

A friend of Speck's tried to interest him in some Utah Copper stock he had bought but now wanted to sell because he was more interested in a Colorado gold mine venture. He and Speck stocked a Manitou hack with liquor and set out to inspect the mine. The driver shared the liquor, which resulted in the hack overturning, smashing every bottle but one. Speck refused to stir another step without refreshments. His friend was in tears at the prospect of losing the Penrose backing. Desperate, he offered to swap his Utah Copper holding (a good-sized block of "doubtful" stock) for funds to finance the gold mine. Penrose still refused. The friend had an inspiration and offered to throw in the remaining bottle. This was something else again. The deal was made.

Finally, on December 30, 1905, the law caught up with Harry Orchard. He was arrested in Caldwell, Idaho, for the bomb murder there of ex-Governor Frank Steunenberg. He confessed many killings, including perhaps eighteen or twenty in the Cripple Creek Mining District. He admitted blowing up the Vindicator Mine in Cripple Creek. During his incarceration, first in Caldwell and later at the state penitentiary in Boise, Orchard was persuaded to turn state's

Harry Orchard was considered one of the most dangerous characters in the country. He was a paid killer whose goal was to murder targeted individuals like Idaho Governor Frank Steunenberg and mine owners such as Speck's friend Charlie MacNeill. During his trial he confessed killing up to twenty victims, just in Cripple Creek alone. Although he was convicted of many crimes and sent to death row, he was never executed and died of old age in prison.
Denver Public Library Western Collection F23318

Charles M. MacNeill, shown here as a young man, became a millionaire at age twenty-eight. He was Speck's close friend and drinking buddy who was also a partner in an assortment of deals, including the Broadmoor Hotel and Utah Copper. Two years younger than Speck, he was once on the hit list of Harry Orchard, a notorious killer. After hours of stalking MacNeill, who was carousing with Speck until the early hours of the morning, Orchard was unable to make his hit and went on to his next victim. Speck would have most certainly perished along with MacNeill had Orchard succeeded in getting his target because his preferred weapon was a bomb.

Courtesy, Pikes Peak Library District.

evidence even though he had admitted to the murder. He implicated the Western Federation of Miners and its top officers for whom he allegedly had been a paid killer. He was thereupon removed from murderer's row in the penitentiary and treated like a prince by prison officials.

What followed was one of the most bizarre episodes in the history of American justice. The Federation's officers were in Denver where no criminal charge was pending against them, so a legal arrest was not possible. The problem of getting them into Idaho to charge them with Governor Steunenberg's murder with Orchard as the principal witness was solved by a conspiracy between Idaho and Colorado officials. Extradition papers were drawn up in Boise against Charles H. Moyer, president; one-eyed, two-fisted William D. Haywood, secretary-treasurer of the Federation; and George Pettibone, formerly active in the miners' union, but now a Denver business man. The three were kidnapped the night of February 17, 1906, and placed aboard a train that headed at top speed for Boise, Idaho.

The renowned Chicago criminal lawyer, Clarence Darrow, was in Boise to be counsel for the defense. William E. Borah, who was to be elected a United States Senator during the protracted trial, joined the forces of the prosecution. Under questioning by Borah, Orchard admitted that in Cripple Creek he had waited a number of nights for Charlie MacNeill, Penrose's pal, with the purpose of killing him, under cover of darkness.

"But you didn't kill him, did you?" asked Darrow. "Why?"

"I never got a chance at him," answered Orchard. "He and Penrose never rolled in until after daylight."

Inasmuch as Orchard's most used weapon was the bomb, it is assumed that a bomb would have killed Penrose as well, had the two been found together.

Brushes with death aside, by this time it was evident that Speck had complete confidence in the Utah Copper project and faith in Daniel Jackling. The copper experiment started making a profit from its first day of operation. Jackling's procedure revolutionized copper mining and made available vast, additional reserves to meet growing world requirements. While the copper group was riding high on copper, Jackling conceived the idea of applying the same process successfully on low-grade gold ore. Alaska Gold was organized — sold at twenty-five cents a share. When the stock reached twenty-seven dollars a share, the canny Penrose served notice on the other members of the pool that he was selling out. He advised them to do the same. When the stock zoomed to thirty-five dollars, they needled him for getting cold feet. Then the operators struck a "horse" — a huge area of barren rock — and the stock collapsed. As far as the members of the group were concerned "the operation was a success but the patient died." Jackling's process was proved successful even though the Alaska Gold stock blew up!

As it became apparent that the new process was proving successful, the Utah Copper stock began to soar. The group staked everything on their ability to handle 5,000 tons of ore a day — an unheardof amount at the time. (They were rolling the dice.) They surpassed this — doubled their goal and quadrupled their profits. They set out to tear down the entire mountain using steam shovels and trains on stepladder levels. Volume was doubled again, then redoubled.

So it was that the three amateurs from Colorado Springs (young men at that) launched the world's largest open face copper mine at Bingham Canyon, and thus gave Utah its biggest single industry. Speck had become a millionaire before age thirty-five with his profits from the real estate, mining, and milling operations. But now in 1905, at age forty, he was a multi-millionaire. And all of this came before the dawn of U.S. income taxes.

CHAPTER XIII

JULIE GETS
HER MAN

B y 1906, it had been a decade since Speck took up residence in Colorado Springs. The cultural temperament of the community had put somewhat of a check on his drinking and other nocturnal activities. Although he did carouse regularly with his business partner MacNeill, there were no boom-town roughnecks to chide Speck about his attire, so fighting in the streets was no longer necessary. He had matured considerably as a businessman.

With this newfound maturity Speck turned into a gadabout. He took frequent trips to the east coast on business and usually, during the hunting season, spent time with his brothers in Montana, Wyoming, and Idaho. He divided his time between Colorado Springs, Salt Lake City, New York City, and Philadelphia. Besides being a member of the El Paso Club in Colorado Springs, he paid dues to the Denver Club, Salt Lake's Alta Club, The Union and University Clubs in New York, and the Philadelphia and Union League Clubs in Philadelphia. When asked why he belonged to so many clubs, Speck reasoned that it was one way of assuring himself of being near an adequate supply of whiskey.

Spencer's boyish good looks became even more striking as he aged. He still wore his trademark boots, breeches, and wide-brimmed hat; and for some occasions he donned his white tie and tails. He indulged himself with the very finest and latest men's fashions. All of this, one would suppose, should have landed him squarely in the midst of the social elite. But he had a number of handicaps.

Speck was not a ladies' man. He was a terrible dancer and a worse conversationalist. In the presence of ladies, he faltered in his speech even in small talk or chit-chat. Of course, he felt comfortable with the girls from the tenderloin, but that was up in the Crik. In Colorado Springs he lived the life of a confirmed bachelor, mixing freely with the members of his El Paso and Cheyenne Mountain Country Clubs. His brothers Boies and Dick were bachelors, the status of which he too chose to remain.

It had been about five years since Speck's first meeting with Mrs. James H. (Julie) McMillan at the clambake that he and Clarence Edsall had hosted at the El Paso Club. She had been born Julie Villiers Lewis, the daughter of the Honorable Alexander Lewis, Detroit's perennial mayor, a member of the Detroit Board of Trade, a director of several banks, and investor in wheat, flour, and real estate. Although he and the other children of the Lewis family were baptized at birth in the Catholic church, their mother brought them up as Episcopalians.

Julie's mother bore thirteen children altogether, although five died in infancy. Of the eight surviving, Julie was the sixth. Since she most resembled her father, she was unceasingly indulged. After attending Miss Brown's School in Boston, she made a Grand Tour of Europe. In 1890, when she returned home, she married Jim McMillan, the boy next door — Yale,

Skull and Bones, rising lawyer, yachtsman, champion golfer, and son of the multimillionaire James McMillan who was the United States Senator from Michigan. This union brought forth two children, Jimmie and Gladys, and for a decade they lived blissfully.

While serving in the Spanish American War in Cuba, McMillan contracted tuberculosis. When he was discharged, Julie took him to Colorado for treatment. They set up residence in a large handsome place off North Cascade Avenue at 30 West Dale Street in Colorado Springs. The treatment was unsuccessful. McMillan died several months after the Edsall-Penrose clambake in 1901. Four years later, her twelve-year-old son Jimmie died of appendicitis.

After recovering from the impact of the death of her husband and her son, Julie decided to stay in Colorado Springs at the Dale Street house which suited her fine. She also decided to marry that very handsome Mr. Penrose who had paid no attention to her at his clambake. A polite friendship grew out of sympathetic concern for her loss. Eventually the friendship transformed into a courtship that continued for almost five years. Julie dazzled Speck with her impervious energy and forthright determination to get what she wanted. But, since she had never been denied anything in her life, this was merely second nature to Julie.

Julie observed Speck's habits as a bachelor and became determined to save him from this awful fate that included burned toast in the morning, an unmade bed, an assortment of rooms in downtown Colorado Springs at the El Paso Club or with bachelors like Horace Devereux, courtships with big horsey women like Sally Halthusen in Cripple Creek, and Lord knows what else.

Noticeably absent in this picture of Spencer Penrose is his traditional western attire including the wide-brimmed hat. Perhaps it was his change of venue from Cripple Creek to Colorado Springs.
Denver Public Library Western Collection. F4683.

Although Julie had not the slightest idea of how to boil an egg or make a bed, she did have the where-with-all to hire someone to handle these tasks for Speck. She sent her help to do Speck's laundry, make his bed and other duties he left undone, and she invited him regularly to breakfast at West Dale Street. And the time came when she told him plainly that his Utah Copper business and his El Paso pool games did not excuse him from escorting her to parties.

This steady diet of being coddled and courted appealed to Speck, so much that he became dependent upon it. Feeling trapped and a bit panic stricken, he talked a bachelor friend of his, Dr. R.N. Keely of Philadelphia, into joining him for an extended trip abroad where he could more properly get the perspective needed to remain happy and single. At the last minute Dick Penrose decided to join them.

On February 6, as the three men took a last glance at the pier where the North German steamer S.S. Lloyd Kaiser Wilhelm der Grosse was ready to pull in its lines, they spotted a small figure, draped in fur, boarding the ship with two companions. Yes, it was Julie McMillan, her daughter Gladys, and a friend from Detroit, Edith Newberry. It looked like the jig was up for Speck.

The plan was that Dick would disembark at Plymouth and board another steamer bound for Cape Town, South Africa, and another geological expedition; Keely and Speck would go on to Cherbourge and then to Paris in Speck's automobile that was to meet them there. It was fairly evident that Julie and party would do the same.

On the second day of the sea voyage, about ninety percent of the passengers were sick. After a rough crossing, Dick bade the group goodbye at Plymouth, and the rest of the party journeyed on to Paris. Keely and Speck planned to leave for the French Riviera shortly thereafter.

Dick's trip to Africa was delayed as indicated by his letter to Dr. Penrose in Philadelphia dated February 12, 1906:

> I had a letter from Speck a couple of days ago. He and Keely got to Paris all right with automobile, and he seems much pleased with it. I believe that they expect to start off on a trip to the South of France in it before long, but I will probably see them in Paris before they start.

According to Dick's diary, he started a trip to Paris on February 22:

> ...on the 11a.m. train from London. The rain has gone and weather perfect. The train to Dover is very crowded because, in addition to the regular number of passengers for France, there are many more on the way to Marseilles to take the P. & O. steamer for the East. I believe it is the Bombay steamer. Crossing the channel was like a mill pond. The boat that took us was the Invicta, one of the new turbine boats, and a wonderfully smooth running little ship. We went from Dover to Calais in just one hour, boarded the train at Calais in a great commotion and rush for seats on the train. The French train was excellent and ran very fast, reaching Paris in about four hours from Calais.
>
> Dr. Keely met me at the station, which was very kind of him as I had no reason to expect him to take the trouble to do so. We drove to the Regina Hotel where I found an excellent room with a bath engaged for me. I had telegraphed ahead to them

to reserve a room with a bath for me. Got dinner with Speck and Keely, and went to bed about midnight.

For the next three days Speck and Keely were joined by Dick in Paris. Finally the two vacationers, itching to get back on the road with Speck's new car, set off for the South of France on a fine and beautiful day. After running about with two lively companions, Dick felt very lonely in Paris at the Regina Hotel even though the accommodations were excellent.

So before departing for England to resume his trip to South Africa, Dick occupied himself with a promise he had made his brother before he departed. That was to compose a letter to Dr. Penrose concerning Julie McMillan. The letter was dated Paris, March 3, 1906:

> I wrote to you last week from London, just before coming here. I found Speck and Keely here and was with them for three or four days, before they started for the South of France in Speck's automobile. I will stay here until the middle of next week, when I will return to London, preparatory to sailing for Africa on March 10th. I was much tempted to go with Speck and Keely to South of France, but after making all arrangements to start for Africa on the 10th I did not want to defer the trip.
>
> Speck has asked me to write to you about a matter concerning which he said he was going to write to you himself. A couple of ladies from Colorado Springs, friends of Speck's, came over from New York on the same boat with us three weeks ago; and they have, at Speck's invitation, gone

south with him in his automobile. One of them is a widow named Mrs. McMillan. Her husband was a son of ex-U.S. Senator McMillan of Michigan. He (her husband) enlisted in the U.S. Army at the beginning of the war with Spain in 1898, contracted fever in Cuba, and later in his weakened condition, contracted consumption, from which he died. Mrs. McMillan is a very good looking and a very agreeable woman of about thirty-five years old, a blonde of medium size. She has one child, a fourteen-year-old girl. She comes originally from Detroit, Michigan, and Speck says that hers is one of the best families there. He says he has known her well for several years. She came here to put her child to school in Switzerland, and the other lady who came with her seems to have come as a sort of companion. I understand that Mrs. McMillan is fairly well off financially and wants to educate her daughter abroad.

Speck seems very much devoted to Mrs. McMillan, and she equally so to him. He has talked to me about proposing marriage to her, and has asked me to write to you about it, and pave the way for him to write to you. Mrs. McMillan seems to understand Speck thoroughly, and the impression I have gotten of her is that she is a thoroughly sensible woman, whom a man ought to get along with if he can get along with any woman whatever. The fact that she is a widow had given her an experience with her first husband that lets her know what men are; and her thirty-five years of age has probably removed all the obnoxious ambitions of many modern women, that she might have had. I doubt, however, if she ever had any, as she seems very sensible.

Speck tells me that for two years, he has carefully considered the proposition of marrying her, and feels that he is not now deciding on a snap judgment, but after due consideration. He seems to have been with her a great deal and to know her thoroughly. Speck is peculiarly situated. He can't read much on account of his eye, and as he himself says, he is not interested in any particular subject that would lead him to seek amusement from literary or scientific sources. He is, therefore, peculiarly dependent on social intercourse. As he himself said to me the other day, he cannot sit down at eight o'clock in the evening and read until bedtime, nor can he go on forever drinking rum at clubs. Therefore he seems to think his only refuge is to get married.

I do not claim to have any wisdom on matrimonial subjects, and I fully realize that I am a damned poor hand to have any advice on such subjects, but I cannot help feeling that Speck would be very much better off if happily married than in his present condition, for reasons which I have just mentioned and which Speck himself gives.

Speck talked to me a good deal about this matter before he left here, though he had never mentioned it to me before we met in Paris. I could of course see, however, that he was very devoted to the lady coming across the ocean. I did not try to influence him one way or the other in his matrimonial desires, but I did advise him strongly, before taking any definite action, to go home when Keely goes, in a few weeks, and see what effect a change of air and surroundings would have on his feelings in the matter. I also told him that if he was bent on getting married, it would be more dignified to go home first and to consummate the deal there, rather than do it here in a foreign land. He said that he had tried going away from the lady for months at a time, but that the separation had no effect on his affection for her. My advice to him, however, to go home first; and if he still wanted to marry the lady, to do so there rather than here, seemed to appeal to him; and when he left here he gave me the impression that he would do so. He will then have a chance to talk to you about the matter. It seems very hard for him to get courage to write to you, because he fears you may think him foolish, but I told him you would do no such thing, and would only give him such advice as you thought best for his own happiness, and he promised me to write to you.

Since he left here in his automobile, I have had a letter saying that he would write to you, and asking me again to be sure and do the same. Hence the cause of this long letter. I hope you will approve of my advice to Speck. As I have said, I am anything but a specialist on matrimony, and it seems comical for anyone to consult me on it, but I have tried to give Speck the best judgment I could.

I will drop a line to you from London before sailing for Africa. My address will, during my absence in Africa, be care of J.S. Morgan & Co., 22 Old Broad Street, London, England.

Three days later Dick set out at last on his geological expedition to Africa, keeping his father posted on his whereabouts and taking great pains to fill him in on all the details of his sea journey to the continent south of Europe.

Dick (R.A.F.) Penrose was clearly Speck's closest brother. From Harvard tutoring arrangements to professional advise on mining possibilities, Dick was always there. He even paved the way with their father to make Speck's marriage an event with total family approval and support. He seemed to have the time and patience to talk things over with Speck and always on a positive level. From a rowdy youngster to a sometimes bombastic and opinionated adult, Dick provided Speck with confidence and comfort. Dick Penrose rose to the top of his profession. Even today the Geological Society of America provides an annual Penrose Award to individuals who make the most important contributions to earth sciences.

Geological Society of America Leadville, Colorado, Museum.

Meanwhile Speck and his touring party were having a delightful time on the Riviera. One day as Julie was sunning herself on the beach, a letter was dropped in her lap from someone behind her — that someone was Speck. The letter was from Dr. Penrose who gave hearty approval of the marriage. That was Speck's proposal. They were married less than a month later on April 26, 1906 in, London at St. George's Church in Hanover. Keely stood up for Speck and Julie's friend, Edith, stood for her. Speck was forty-one. Julie was thirty-five. It was an unusually happy union.

Speck cabled Dick who replied with his warm congratulations and this letter, dated May 1, 1906 to Dr. Penrose:

I am glad you feel so favorably about Speck's matrimonial matter. Since my arrival here, I have received a cablegram from him telling me of his marriage in London, and I have replied by cable sending my congratulations to him and his wife. I hope he is going to be happy as he himself said to me in Paris, he has not gone into this matter hastily, but after several years acquaintance with the lady so they ought both to know their own minds. If I had known Speck was going to be married so soon and in London, I would have delayed my trip to Africa to help him out at his marriage, but I thought I would probably be back in time.

He wasn't kidding when he said they had "not gone into this matter hastily." It had been over five years since Speck first met Julie. If they did not know everything about one another by this time, it was no one's fault but their own.

From London the newlyweds headed for Paris and took an apartment at the Princess Hotel. A few days later Dick arrived in Venice on a steamer from Africa. On June 4, he reported to his father that "Speck and his wife seem to be very happy. Both look first rate and seem to be having a good time."

The newlyweds soon set out on a several weeks trip to Tours and Vichy in their automobile.

CHAPTER XIV

WHEELING
AND DEALING

❖

Speck's marriage was the beginning of a new life for him. His playboy days were over. Back in Colorado Springs, Mr. and Mrs. Penrose made her mansion at 30 West Dale Avenue their home.

One of Speck's first business dealings upon returning from his honeymoon was to set final arrangements for selling the mill trust. Before the sale in 1907 to the Guggenheims, it had paid a handsome $2,190,014 in dividends.

By this time Speck had bought or built the Cripple Creek Sampling and Ore Company; the National Gold Extraction Company in Goldfield; the Standard Milling and Smelting Company; the Colorado-Philadelphia Reduction Company in Colorado City; the U.S. Reduction Company; and the famous Short Line, a scenic narrow-gauge railroad from Cripple Creek to Colorado City. He was also a director of the First National Bank of Colorado Springs, Colorado Title and Trust Company in Colorado Springs, the Cripple Creek Railroad, Grand Junction and Grand Valley Railroad, and the International Trust Company of Denver.

Charles "Tal" Penrose was Speck's only brother to follow in his father's footsteps. Tal, after graduating first in his class at Harvard, was a constant source of pride for the family. Dr. R. A.F. Penrose was also delighted that Tal developed his medical practice in Philadelphia where he remained in close touch with his father.
R.L. Olson Personal Collection

In an effort to "get away with the boys," Speck scheduled a Montana hunting trip in September 1907 with his brothers Boies and Tal. During the hunting expedition, Tal had a close-to-death encounter with a large brown bear. Only the fact that he was a doctor and knew the exact nature of his injuries, was he able to save himself. Dick mentions the accident in a letter to his father dated October 7, 1907: "Tal was apparently injured badly during that hunting trip in September but he was revived and will have no serious trouble with his wounds. From what I have heard, it was about as narrow an escape as ever a man has had."

In the late fall of the same year, Speck and Julie took a short trip to Europe where they toured Germany for a short while, were joined briefly by Dick Penrose, then returned home. By this time Speck was the largest stockholder in Utah Copper. He, Jackling and MacNeill did not stop with this venture, but went on to organize the Chino Copper Company in Arizona and Ray Consolidated in New Mexico.

In 1908, at age forty-two, Penrose became interested in doing something else with the good earth besides digging for gold and copper. He developed fruit orchards about twenty miles south of Colorado Springs, where he envisioned a thriving community. He brought water from nearby Beaver Creek for a municipal water system, and built a rail connection with the Denver & Rio Grande Railroad at a cost of over $500,000. The grateful residents named the town Penrose, Colorado, in his honor.

For $100,000, Speck built the Beaver-Penrose & Northern Railroad, which ran from a point on the Royal Gorge to Penrose, Colorado, over seven miles of track, with a steam locomotive and passenger coach. One of the rail cars was made out of a Stevens-Duryea Brougham once owned by Speck.

Speck's father died on December 13, 1908, at the age of eighty-one. This depressed Speck for some time because he was not sure that he had ever risen in his father's graces to the same level as his older brothers despite his successes. The passing of Dr. Penrose marked the end of a long subtle dispute between father and son. Speck seemed to have been subconsciously driven to push just a little bit harder and do a little bit better on everything he attempted with the secret hope that someday word would eventually get back to his father of his accomplishments. Dr. Penrose, to his dying day, had been openly disappointed, apprehensive, and suspect of Speck, even after his son's financial successes. Speck and Dr. Penrose were constantly at odds with each other, truly a case of a permanent clash between father and son.

Early the following year, January 21, 1909, Speck lost his boyhood chum and the business associate most responsible for his success, when Charles L. Tutt died suddenly of a heart attack at the age of forty-five in a New York hotel. Tutt was a millionaire at the age of thirty-five. After his retirement from the mountains, he spent most of his time at his summer place in Oregon, where he kept his forty-two-foot cabin cruiser, "Anemone." The friendship and mutual respect between Tutt and Penrose had grown strong over the years, and Speck took the untimely loss of his long-time partner extremely hard. Some say he turned his lost affection toward Charles Tutt Jr. after the death of the older Tutt.

Just two months later on March 13, General Palmer, the Civil War hero, railroad builder, and founder of Colorado Springs, died at age seventy.

By 1910, the Penrose family had attained a rare distinction. Spencer Penrose was listed in "Who's Who in America," which meant that now Dr. Penrose and all of his oldest surviving sons, Boies, Tal, Dick, and Speck, had achieved this honor. It was a personal disappointment to Speck, however, since his father could not be alive to bask in what would have obviously been surprise and satisfaction.

Speck bought the Turkey Creek Ranch in 1911. It was the largest ranch property he could find in central Colorado. He stocked it with the best purebred Holstein cattle and exotic sheep he could find in mid-western stock country. That same year he also pioneered the sugar beet industry in western Kansas. But the principal focal point of Speck's interest continued to center on Cripple Creek, where he revitalized three gold mines and continued to extract millions. Speck's wealth and backing made Bert Carlton, his close friend, the business king of Cripple Creek in the period after 1911. Because he wound up controlling the majority of the mining interests of Cripple Creek, Carlton, a millionaire at thirty-three, was now called "King Bert." Harry Gehm, a wise old-timer from Cripple Creek, made a sage comment on the Crik that seems to sum it up, "Bob Womack discovered the place, Stratton was its beacon light in the boom days, and A.E. Carlton was its heartbeat."

By 1912, attorney Henry Blackmer, considered "smoother than oil, sharper than a razor, and the most brilliant of the Cripple Creek crowd," gave up his Cripple Creek interest — which at one time included owning the Midland-Terminal Railroad — to invest in Wyoming oil with Verner Reed. Expatriate Reed had stayed in Paris for a lively thirteen years and made world news by driving an underslung Panhard across the Sahara Desert. He came back to Denver to join his old Socialite drinking partner, Blackmer, for the Wyoming oil scheme, and to promote Denver as the second oil capital of the nation.

By this time Penrose had become a headline maker himself and he loved it. It fanned his immense ego and he was beginning to show signs of becoming a showman. The almost-whispering voice for which the big man from Philadelphia had once been known had become a bombastic bellow sprinkled generously with profanity. Although Speck was stronger than ever, he was no longer referred to as the "strong silent type." Civic-minded Penrose spent some of his considerable wealth in improving his community. He made it possible for millions of Colorado Springs visitors to ascend Pikes Peak without walking. He built an automobile road at a cost of more than one million dollars and gave it to the U.S. government. Later, he bought the defunct cog rail road to the peak's summit and put it into successful operation.

The sinking of the Titanic in 1912 on the North Atlantic drew concerned attention from Julie and Speck Penrose since they had made so many crossings. However, it did not deter them from attending the wedding of Julie's daughter, Gladys McMillan, to Count Cornet du Ways Ruart of Belgium in 1914.

Later that year while Speck, then forty-eight, was helping Carlton draw as much wealth out of Cripple Creek as possible, a fortuitous hiring took place. A stout young itinerant from Manassa, Utah, went to work as a mucker in the Portland Mine at the suggestion and invitation of his older brother.

This fellow, William Harrison, ninth of eleven children, had had some experience in prizefighting and, along with his brother, Bernie, was receptive to an idea of a boxing match with the town's "young white hope," George Coplen — a strapping giant heavyweight with the power of a steam shovel. Bernie Harrison was willing to don the gloves himself until he took his first look at Coplen. At this point he touted his younger brother to take his place. Since both of the Harrison boys were heavyweights and both fought under the name of "Jack Dempsey," a name they borrowed from the *Police Gazette*, no one was the wiser.

Prior to the "Jack Dempsey-George Coplen" match which drew wide-spread notoriety, both men trained in the back rooms of two prominent saloons on Bennett Avenue — Jack Dempsey at the Divide, George Coplen at the Golden Nugget. Needless to say, this stimulated business, drawing curious crowds where one had to punch his way into the saloon, then elbow his way to the bar and back room.

The event was scheduled to take place on September 3, 1915, at the Cripple Creek Opera House. When the big day arrived, seats were at a premium and standing room was not available. However, Speck and Charlie MacNeill, who

*In 1915, Speck and his friends promoted a prizefight in
Cripple Creek between George Coplen and Jack Dempsey. On
September 3, the fight was held in the Opera House before a
standing-room-only crowd. Coplen, who Cripple Creek fans
called their "Young White Hope," went seven grueling rounds
with newcomer Dempsey, pegged as the "Manassa Mauler."
Seeing both opponents were ready to drop from exhaustion the
referee finally called a decision in favor of Dempsey, who soon
became Heavyweight Champion of the World. The rest is history.*
Denver Public Library Western Collection. F21490

had helped to promote the fight, had ringside seats. The fight was a grueling battle. At one point it looked like Demspey was a goner. Coplen nearly stopped him with the first punch of the second round. Dempsey said, "For a second I thought the building had blown up under my feet." At the end of the seventh round, Dempsey said he learned that not all fights are won with fists. About to drop from exhaustion himself, Dempsey said to the referee, "What do you want me to do, kill this fellow?" The referee looked at Coplen, who was shaky but still on his feet, and awarded the contest to Dempsey. It was after this fight that the younger Harrison decided to take up the prizefighting ring seriously. His first step was to leave the mines and head back to his home state of Utah. The balance of the Manassa Mauler's ring career is history.

In addition to helping to promote the Dempsey-Coplen fight, Speck was busy dealing with his wide assortment of interests. Among them was the Golden Cycle Mining and Reduction Company in which he invested heavily before the sale of the U.S. Reduction Company to the Guggenheims. On April 29, 1915, a scandalous article appeared in the local papers stating that Penrose and MacNeill, both deeply involved financially in Golden Cycle were, as former owners of U.S. Reduction, promoting a scheme to wreck their former company. The accusation was that Penrose had abandoned plants of the U.S. Reduction Company and leased the property to Golden Cycle before the "sell and buy" transaction was made. Litigation on this lasted for some time, but the outcome ultimately was in favor of the Penrose interests, despite the fact that the Guggenheims had hired all of the big guns of the legal profession to formally charge Penrose.

While touring Europe in October of that same year, Herbert Hoover, who was a good friend of Dick Penrose, visited Speck's step daughter Gladys, a Belgian Countess. The friendship between Dick and Hoover grew to a lasting relationship. Speck, after his brother's death, continued to remain friendly with the future president.

CHAPTER XV

POURTALES' CASINO
MARKS THE SPOT

I n 1885, Count James de Pourtales from Silesia bought
interest in the Willcox dairy farm at the foot of Cheyenne Mountain south of Colorado Springs. Wanting to make
enough money through land speculation to restore his family
estate in Prussia, the Count increased his holdings to 2,400
acres and announced the establishment of a beautiful residential area, which he called "the community of Broadmoor."
The name was an anglicized version of "breitmoor" or "wide
wasteland," because prior to the land development, the area
was filled with scrub oak, underbrush, and cacti.

Using an artificial lake, Pourtales was able to landscape
and irrigate the property. He platted lots and laid out streets;
and in 1891, he built a spacious casino on the rim of the lake
modeled after the Imperial Palace at Potsdam, Germany. His
plan was to turn the area into an American Monte Carlo where
patrons could drink, wine and dine, dance, and throw dice.

The Count had convinced Colorado Springs to extend
its trolley car line to include his Broadmoor area so it actually became a part of the city. Pourtales planned to build a
fine hotel directly across the lake from his casino, but, due

to fluxuating and unsettled international business conditions and local opposition to gambling, his hotel was never built. He held the property until the '93 Panic when his debts reached $450,000. Pourtales let the casino pass into receivership, and it burned to the ground on July 19, 1897.

In 1898, the second casino was built along with the first Broadmoor Hotel, which had accommodations for 100 guests. In 1906, the property was foreclosed on by a Scottish syndicate and reverted to the Stratton Estate and remained idle for years. At one time the little hotel was used as a boarding school for girls, and later as a hotel on lease.

Some years later, Penrose was elected president of the El Paso Club. Founded in 1878, it was one of the oldest such clubs in the West to "furnish billiards, cards, and reading rooms for the enjoyment of the professional and business men who belong." By this time, 1916, Speck had acquired considerable land in the Broadmoor area, including most of that originally owned by Pourtales.

That same year, the Penroses decided to move into an area above the Broadmoor. Their Dale Street home was temporarily occupied by W. F. Moore, a Philadelphia millionaire, and later loaned to the Broadmoor Art Academy.

They bought a one-story Mediterranean villa from Captain and Mrs. Ashton Potter who had built the mansion in 1910. Because it was situated in the middle of an apple orchard (el pomar in Spanish), the name of the area became known as El Pomar. Speck added a second and third floor, enlarging the villa to a total of thirty rooms with many bedrooms and sitting rooms. There were seven bedrooms on the first floor alone. Through the double front doors, one entered a tiled foyer from which a magnificent dining room was visible. Here, lavish parties were held and dinners served on a table that was nine yards long. Above the massive table hung a spectacular chandelier that Speck had bought as an anniversary gift for Julie. The library walls were beautifully carved oak. For his own suite, Speck designed a huge second-story picture window facing southwest to capture the beauty of Cheyenne Mountain with which he was particularly intrigued. He placed his favorite chair in front of the window, assuring himself an unobstructed view of his surroundings. Adjoining his bedroom was an exercise room where he stored all of the latest equipment.

Speck continued to acquire more Broadmoor acreage. Eventually amassing a total of 400 acres, he closed the deal for $90,000 cash. In the back of his mind, for several years prior to 1916, was a plan for a huge resort hotel, something bigger and better than he had seen in Europe and elsewhere on his many tours abroad.

In 1916, the Antlers Hotel was considered the number one hotel in Colorado Springs and one of the best in Colorado. Built by General Palmer, the historic hotel had burned down at one time but had been rebuilt. Billy Dunning, a favorite of Penrose and MacNeill, had managed the Antlers since 1901. However, in the spring of 1916, George Krause, manager the Palmer Estate, fired Dunning.

On May 12, 1916, the press announced that the two Colorado Springs multi-millionaires, Penrose and MacNeill, were going to build "the most wonderful hotel in the west — the most wonderful in the United States" and would install Billy Dunning as its manager. The headline of the article stated, "Capitalists will get even with the Palmer Estate for letting 'First Citizen' of the Springs out at Antlers."

About the same time a *Denver Post* story said, "Whatever form it finally takes the new hotel that Penrose and MacNeill will build will easily surpass anything in the west. It will be especially designed to catch the year-around trade of wealthy families. There will be a golf course and polo grounds, a lake, skating rink with an artificial ice plant so that there can be ice skating year around."

In discussing his firing with MacNeill, Dunning said, "I'll say this for the Antlers, it's a great hotel and a fine memorial to General Palmer."

MacNeill returned this blustering comment, "Memorial! Blazes! I'll spend one million dollars out of my own pocket and build a bigger memorial to you, Billy."

The newspaper announcement went on to predict that the Cheyenne Mountain area would become the mecca of the wealthy families of the country who now flock to Coronado Beach and Palm Beach. The new hotel was to cost $1,000,000 and would be built on the site of the first Pourtales casino.

Speck hired several designers before he was satisfied. Finally, Whitney Warren, designer of New York's Grand Central Station, the Ritz, and Biltmore hotels, was selected to be the architect. Despite World War I's demand of the war for materials, construction of the Broadmoor began on April 13, 1916. Stewart Construction Company got the building contract. Crews as large as 500 worked on the building at one time. It was built in the architectural style of the Italian Renaissance, with Italian craftsmen installing many of its features. The exterior was pink stucco. Julie took an active role in selecting art objects and furnishings from Paris to Hong Kong. Charles Tutt Jr., the son of Speck's former partner, joined Penrose in a supervisory capacity as the Broadmoor was being built. That summer the casino was moved to the south shore of the lake where its new identity became a golf club.

Meanwhile there was action on the political front. By the time the local members of the Grand Old Party gathered to elect delegates for the national convention, Penrose had become a unanimous choice to take the July trip. He was elected and became an influential member of the Colorado delegation that nominated Charles Evans Hughes to the GOP's top spot.

Being on the inside of the political wheeling and dealings and certainly under the heavy influence of his older brother, the senior U.S. Senator from the state of Pennsylvania, fifty-year-old Speck had strong feelings about the presidential election. So strong in fact, that he bet $175,000 that Hughes would win. When Woodrow Wilson captured the office on November 9, 1917, for a second term, Speck paid off his bet with mumbling undertones about the inadequacies of the electoral college.

In 1917, while his Broadmoor was being built, Penrose threw his boundless energy, time, and money into every patriotic home-front war effort to which he was called. Speck was unlike his older brother Boies, who, through Dick Penrose, was approached by Herbert Hoover, then chairman of the Belgian Relief Committee, for support of the operation. Boies not only declined but developed a considerable vein of personal opposition.

During that year the American Red Cross gave Colorado Springs a quota of $100,000 in its $100,000,000 fund drive. Because of his affluence and interest, Penrose was appointed general chairman. He promptly doubled the quota by raising $217,000 — the highest per capita contribution of any American city.

From the beginning of the fund-raising campaign Speck held the title "unafraid." He was quoted as saying, "we probably will have to come through more than once for the Red Cross funds. The next time I will give more. The next time more again. And, if it takes the shirt off my back before the thing is finished, they can have that, too!" With this declaration and a cash donation of $40,000, Speck brought one hundred of his fellow campaign workers at a banquet in the Antlers Hotel to their feet. Speck promised the dividends to the Red Cross from his heavy holdings in Utah Copper, Chino Copper, Ray Consolidated, United Verde Extension, and United States Steel. During the banquet Penrose publicly castigated two of his fellow millionaires for their penury in giving and tagged them "tight-wads."

By the time the Broadmoor (now called the "pleasure palace" by the press) was finished, Penrose had added so much during its construction that the total cost exceeded $3,100,000. While the world was gripped in the final throes of the Great War, the time for the Broadmoor's grand opening was set for Saturday, June 29, 1918, and all arrangements were in the grand Penrose manner. It was to be a "big blow out" according to Speck, and that it was. He invited local friends, social leaders, and dignitaries from all over the country. Colorado Springs guests included William S. Jackson, William Lennox, Oliver H. Shoup, Bernie H. Hopkins, Charles L. Tutt Jr., James F. Burns, and V.Z. Reed. Guests were drawn from all directions using Lake Avenue trolley cars, Stanley Steamers, and elegant carriages with blue-blooded horses. There was a party at the indoor pool, fifty riding horses available, and seals and flamingos in the lake. To add a little highlight to the function, the flamingos, specially trained to stand knee deep in the lake and look ornamental, joined the party on the veranda and terrace, and the seals got loose in the lobby. Two orchestras played in the crystal chandelier-lit ballroom.

More than 200 of the nation's socially elite were served from a menu that included a dessert named in honor of Julie's granddaughter.

MENU
Broadmoor Trout au Bleu
Braised Sweetbreads aux Perles du Perigord
Boneless Royal Squab
Souffle Glace
Courtesse de Cornet

Since it was wartime, and Hollywood celebrities were out canvassing the country selling Liberty Bonds and were therefore unavailable, Penrose, searching for the perfect "first guest" at his Broadmoor Hotel, looked to the number one business name in the business world. He invited John D. Rockefeller Jr., who came and registered as the first guest. However, after taking one whiff of the new paint smell, the highly allergic Rockefeller left the fabulous new hotel and registered at the Antlers. This was a humiliation that Speck had the good humor to soon forget in the spirit of "so what, the Broadmoor will have important guests by the thousands."

Penrose continued to expand the hotel. He added a polo field, bridle-paths, hiking trails, stables for 400 mounts, tennis courts, an indoor ice skating rink, rustic buildings, a golf course and shelters for the golfers, a reservoir, a zoo, a riding academy, and much more.

There are many stories about why Speck had the "a" in Broadmoor raised higher than the other letters and had this distinctive design registered as the hotel's trademark. The most widely accepted is the tale that it was symbolic of his beloved Cheyenne Mountain or Pikes Peak. Another was that since the adjoining Broadmoor area had nothing

Two years after its spectacular opening on June 29, 1918, the Broadmoor Hotel already looked like a permanent fixture. Guests marveled at the stunning view from the west side of the structure in front of the lake looking up at the breathtaking Rocky Mountain Front Range.
Courtesy, Pikes Peak Library District.

to do with the hotel itself, Penrose wanted to have a special trademark fashioned to set apart his hotel's name from the surrounding residential area. Still another was that Speck's secretary made a mistake in a letter that he okayed! And, a popular legend that persists is that Speck was once thrown out of the Antlers when he entered on horseback, so he took the "a" out of Broadmoor in opposition to the Antlers.

Around this time, Julie's granddaughter, Baroness Pauline, became deathly ill, and Julie promised that "if she gets well, I'll become a Catholic again." She got well! Not too long after that Julie built the Pauline Chapel behind the Broadmoor.

Speck gave hundreds of thousands of dollars in contributions to such organizations as the Belgian Relief, YMCA, and others. In early March of 1918, in another gesture of patriotism, Penrose gave their 30 West Dale Street home, previously occupied by the Broadmoor Art Academy, to the War Department as a rehabilitation center for sick and wounded officers, and he paid the one million dollar medical costs of the program. The Dale Street property was big enough to house sixty officers, and had a modern kitchen, baths, a swimming pool, billiard room, and conservatory. In October his offer was accepted, and before long his former home was overflowing with wounded French soldiers fresh from the Western Front.

While Speck nurtured his patriotism by his generous offers to his country, the U.S. government dealt him one of its hardest blows. In 1918, a proposed law prohibiting alcoholic beverages was introduced to Congress. This was like a personal attack against one of Penrose's most cherished freedoms — a freedom he would not readily relinquish.

On April 26, 1919, the Baroness Pauline de Selys, Julie's four-year-old granddaughter, dressed up in her Belgian peasant costume. This scene is from a street parade in Colorado Springs to celebrate the returning soldiers from the Western Front. Soon after, the Baroness became extremely sick. Julie said, "if she gets well I'll become a Catholic again!" She got well and not too long after that Julie built the Pauline Chapel behind the Broadmoor.
Courtesy, Pikes Peak Library District.

CHAPTER XVI
THE PROHIBITION NIGHTMARE

O ne could not say that the Penroses were dipsomaniacs, but they did do their share of social drinking and liked it. Even Julie Penrose imbibed at El Pomar with a dry sherry before dinner, while Speck downed a shot of straight whiskey — a habit he had picked up during those early days in Cripple Creek with side kick Charlie MacNeill.

In 1919, when the Wilson Administration was presented with the Volstead Prohibition Enforcement Act, the nation was fed up with the wild and frolicking days of free-flowing gin, five-cent beers, and the huge assortment of drunks who failed to support their families, beat their wives, and were generally out-for-no-good as a result of excessive alcoholic beverage consumption.

Speck was forewarned about prohibition by Congress' earlier consideration of the 18th Amendment. When prohibition became imminent, he took a bold precautionary measure against a drought that might last a lifetime by constructing the largest wine cellar in western America. Speck stocked it with liquor that came in freight car lots, and unloaded it from the Rio Grande with armed guards

standing by. Two carloads came from his New York apart-
ment; two from cellars of the Penrose sugar plantation in
Hawaii; 1,000 cases from Charles and Company in New
York City; and the entire bar stock was purchased from the
Brown Palace Hotel in Denver and other similar setups in
Philadelphia. He stocked his cellar with the finest wines and
liquors from two continents. It became the largest private
stock of alcoholic beverages in the country, second only to
that of Secretary of Treasury Andrew Mellon of Pittsburgh.
But Mellon was richer and owned Old Overholt Distilleries.
In addition to the vast supply stored in a subterranean tunnel
under the artificial lake on the Broadmoor grounds, Speck
leased two large rooms in the University Club of New York,
which he filled with this contraband.

On July 4, 1919, Speck went to Toledo, Ohio, to see
his friend Jack Dempsey defeat Jess Willard in their historic
heavyweight championship fight. Speck's presence at ringside with his cronies is documented in a mural of the famous
fight done by artist James Montgomery Flagg for Dempsey's
restaurant in New York.

An example of how Dick and Boies Penrose felt about
prohibition is best illustrated by this letter dated October
29, 1919, from Dick in Philadelphia to Boies at the Senate
Chambers in Washington:

Dear Boies: I want to congratulate you on being
one of the few Republicans who voted to sustain
the President's veto of the prohibition enforcement
act. This inequitable act passed Congress under
shamefully strong Republican support; it is a pomp
and verbose document of over fifty pages, written
in such a puerile, hysterical and intolerant manner
that of necessity it disgusts every normal minded

person. Inquisitions of the Middle Ages could not have been drawn up in a more vindictive document.

Will the Republican Party never come to its senses? You must look beyond boundaries of the narrow intellects of the prejudiced leaders to feel the pulse of the American people, and if the Republican Party cannot acquire this broad vision they are courting defeat. I travel considerably and meet different classes of people, so that I know that prohibition today, outside of the small but very well organized minority, is disgusting and repellent to the vast majority of the American people. What we need is less infringement on the rights of man and more of the liberty and freedom for which the Republican Party once stood. If this party is going to try to crush people to the level of what was once the status of Russian serfs under the pretext of establishing a modern Utopia, I believe they will have hard sledding at the next election. Today they are receiving the blame for prohibition and the Democrats are laughing up their sleeves. Your affectionate brother, R.A.F. Penrose, Jr.

Back in Colorado Springs, Speck and Julie continued to live their privileged life and were often seen in "his" and "her" Loziers, twin canary-yellow touring cars. The idea of drinking in public places never occurred to Speck, so he solved this problem by becoming a member of more clubs strategically located around the country.

Penrose became one of the country's most vociferous opponents of the prohibition law. He assailed it as an infringement on the personal liberties guaranteed by the constitution. And, while his hard drinking days were over, he nonetheless wanted a certain amount of freedom for himself and his friends to take a drink whenever the spirit moved them. Speck was getting hard-boiled and his language frequently was punctuated with four-letter words. Perhaps Speck felt that this was the only way he could make himself heard.

In Colorado, the wet and dry forces were beginning to show signs of greater strength on both sides. The Women's Christian Temperance Union (WCTU) headed by Mrs. Adrianna Hungerford of Denver and the Anti-Saloon League of Colorado led by the Reverend A.J. Finch represented the "dries." Speck took up the cause of the opposition with the American Liberty League.

On October 31, 1925, Speck became the Colorado chairman of the American Liberty League, which was dedicated to repeal of the 18th Amendment. He launched a bitter political attack on prohibition, locking horns with both the WCTU and the Anti-Saloon League. Whenever he was interviewed by the press he never failed to take a verbal swing at prohibition. His League sought legislative changes in the Volstead Act by electing congressmen opposed to prohibition, and he actively carried on the campaign. Speck bitterly attacked "weak-spined" individuals who were "privately wet and publicly dry" and declared he would recruit 10,000 new members to the League in Colorado. He pointed out that 8,000 people were blinded by bad liquor in 1924 and that millions of dollars were being spent to keep out the one percent of pure liquor consumed. "I am not in favor of saloons, and I am for temperance, but I will never vote for a prohibitionist," declared Speck in a newspaper interview.

The announcement of Speck as head of the American Liberty League brought lengthy statements from "dry" headquarters, "While we may not command so many dollars for our cause as do the 'wets' for theirs, we are still on the job and expect to remain there, not only the WCTU forces, but many thousands of red-blooded American citizens." In publicity sent out from state headquarters, the Colorado WCTU said, "We cannot but admire Spencer Penrose for the open stand he has taken concerning the campaign to be launched in Colorado." Speck received constant denunciation from the pulpit because of his leadership on repeal of prohibition, but he worked hard writing letters, contributing money, founding and joining organizations, and probably praying.

Early in 1926, *The Denver Post* launched an opinion poll on prohibition, calling it the *"Denver Post's* Rocky Mountain Referendum on Prohibition." A full page article including the "ballot" stated that "The dries and the wets are girding their loins for the fray..." and called for a vote. The poll offered the voters "against" prohibition a chance to permit sale of light wines and beer under government supervision. Judges for the ballot were carefully selected. In addition to leaders of both wets and dries, Mrs. Hungerford and Speck Penrose, they included Claude K. Boettcher of Denver's Boettcher and Company, investment bankers; Fred Farrar, general counsel for Colorado from Denver; Colonel Patrick J. Hamrock, a Denver veteran of World War I and former Adjutant General of Colorado; and Oliver M. Shoup, former Governor of Colorado from Colorado Springs. The article billed Speck as president of the Broadmoor Hotel Company and builder of the famous Pikes Peak auto highway and Cheyenne Mountain Highway.

Speck's argument for the wets appeared on a full page of the *Denver Post:*

Face the facts! Prohibition and Volsteadism are the issue, not temperance and the saloon. I am for temperance and am against the return of the saloon, as are all-right thinking men, but when you face the facts as they exist, not as they are painted by many prohibitionists, but as they really are in all parts of the United States, you cannot help but realize that prohibition is not only a failure but a menace.

People don't believe in the law and they have no regard for it. The climax has been reached in the east where the law is violated openly. That is admitted. There is no such thing as temperance now. Distilled liquors, mostly poisonous, have taken the place of wine and beer. Even church surveys show this.

The Volstead law has been tried for six years and has been convicted. It is no longer a moral issue. It is one of decency. Two years ago many people would have rejected the suggestion that the Volstead law was not virtually sacred in character. To question the merit of the existing prohibition enforcement legislation would have been to advocate unbridled crime and vice. But now there is increasing evidence everywhere against Volsteadism as a breeder of a host of evils which a few years ago were not known in American life; i.e., bootlegging, bribery, corruption, widespread drinking among youth of both sexes and almost universal disrespect for law.

The report of the Federal Council of Churches and the more recent declaration of the Church Temperance Society of the Protestant Episcopal Church both found the present methods of legislation wanting and in the latter a direct demand was made for modification of the present laws so as to permit the manufacturer and use of beer and light wines.

The trouble with the prohibition situation is that men are afraid to speak out the truth that is in their hearts. Politicians vote dry and act wet. Businessmen, knowing the truth of all the evils of prohibition, have been afraid to admit it publicly. But times are changing — anyone with eyes and ears open knows it. Ask the policeman, the district attorney, the reporters, the physicians, and the men of other professions if they think that prohibition is a success. They'll tell you no, if they speak from their hearts.

The shift in sentiment in the United States during the last year as a result of the wider knowledge of the evils of Volsteadism is significant. The people are coming to their senses.

The vote on *The Denver Post* poll was about 2-to-1 in favor of the more lenient attitude toward prohibition. But this was merely a newspaper campaign and greater frustration was about the only result for the Penrose forces.

Early in 1927, the drys, including protestant church groups, thought for a moment that they had the battling Penrose on the ropes. From southern France, where he had just purchased a chateau with a large vineyard, he wrote his attorney Henry McAllister in Denver that he had decided to take the advise of his friend F.G. Bonfils, publisher of *The Denver Post*, and give up his fight against prohibition:

> Mr. Bonfils had advised me time and again to quit fighting the Prohibitionists and I believe I will take his advice. I am readily coming to the conclusion that the people of Colorado and the U.S.A. are such fools as to kill themselves on ice water and

bootlegged liquor. Perhaps the best thing to do is to leave them alone and look out for ourselves.

I believe in safety first and when the ship is sinking it is a case of everyone for himself. Therefore, I think it will be better for me to spend a large part of my time in Europe where a person has some freedom and can live as he pleases so long as he does not interfere with the rights of other people. For these reasons I want to get a vineyard so as to produce the juice of the grape which has always pleased mankind and even the gods. Wine is a product of nature and I do not believe that the good Lord would have permitted fermentation if he thought the results of fermentation would be harmful to man.

I am in fine shape and busy all the time, doing nothing.

In a joint venture between Speck and his Cripple Creek friend Henry M. Blackmer, former president of Midwest Refining Company of Denver and tentatively out of the country to avoid testifying in the "Teapot Dome" scandal, they bought Chateau De Gravis, just thirty miles from Bordeaux. It was located in an area where vineyards produced up to 1800 barrels of wine a year, and considered a favorite in England for the previous fifty years.

"I am very pleased to get the chateau as it fully comes up to my expectations and I believe it will be a very good place for my friends to come and visit whenever they feel like doing so," Speck told McAllister in another letter.

After winding up their business in Bordeaux, the Penroses took an extended tour to St. Moritz, Morocco, Algiers, and Genoa, then returned to the Broadmoor. Back home again the "champion of the anti-Prohibitionists" resumed his battle against the offensive law with increased vigor.

During the 1928 presidential campaign, Speck publicly supported Democrat Al Smith against Herbert Hoover because Smith favored repeal and Hoover did not. Naturally, Speck was one of Colorado's fifteen repeal delegates at the national convention in 1928. From time to time during his tireless campaign for repeal of prohibition, Penrose could be seen wearing an Al Smith brown derby while driving his pet llama from a special two-wheel "Repeal" rig at Repeal Headquarters.

By the time the 18th Amendment was repealed on December 5, 1933, Penrose had contributed several hundred thousand dollars to organizations that had fought for repeal during the previous fourteen years. With repeal, Speck felt that the one personal liberty he cherished the most was finally legally restored. His collection of private stock built during prohibition was put on public display — perhaps a symbolic gesture to show the world his bitter and lasting resentment of the prohibition law.

CHAPTER XVII

INN KEEPER OF
THE WORLD

En route home after a European trip early in 1920, Julie
and Speck Penrose were recognized by a prominent New
York hotel man as they walked up Fifth Avenue. The local
man summoned the leaders of the industry who hurriedly
planned an elaborate banquet in Speck's honor, in appreciation of the fact that his Broadmoor Hotel had contributed
to the hotel industry. The centerpiece was a replica of the
Broadmoor.

Speck, now fifty-four years old, reciprocated in the grand
Penrose style. He invited the leading east and west coast hotel
executives and a few from points in between — seventy in
number — to be his guests for a week at the Broadmoor. They
traveled in style, luxury, and comfort in three private Rock
Island Pullman railroad cars — one from the Pacific coast.
They were to be entertained during the first week of September 1920. A *Denver Post* headline read: "Colorado Springs
Multimillionaire Brings Half Billion Dollars' Worth of Eastern
and Western Hotel Men to Colorado for a Week's Stay."

Among the more notable guests to be invited were Senator James J. Walker of New York City, who later became that

city's mayor; John Ringling of the popular Ringling Brothers Circus; and Oscar Tschirky of the Waldorf.

On July 17, the *Denver Post* reported:

A special train will leave New York City the latter part of August bearing hotel managers of New York, Newport, and Atlantic City en route to Colorado Springs to spend a week as guests of Spencer Penrose at the Broadmoor Hotel when the most elaborate entertainment ever staged in Colorado will be afforded.

And Penrose is going to pay for the entire trip, special train and all. Dinners, dances, automobile and aeroplane races, polo, and numerous private parties are on the program for the entertainment.

All of this is because when Penrose was in New York City bound for Colorado Springs after his trip to Europe, a New York hotel man found him and staged an elaborate banquet for him, had a model of the new Broadmoor made for the centerpiece and left nothing undone for the newest of internationally-known hotel owners. And now Penrose is going the outfit one better.

In addition to the New York men he will have as his guests a number of Californians high up in the hotel world.

The list of guests from New York includes:

A.M. Adams, 1480 Broadway
Jack Ball, 1480 Broadway
Harry Barth, 36 Cooper Square
Robert D. Blackman, Hotel Belleclair, Broadway & 77th Street
John Mc. E. Bowman, Hotel Biltmore

George C. Brown, Park Avenue Hotel
Clark E. Eaton, 165 Broadway, Mgr. American
Car & Foundry Company
William H. Edwards, Collector,
N.Y. Custom House
Charles E. Gehring, 1480 Broadway,
N.Y. Hotel Review
Thomas D. Green, Hotel Woodward,
55th & Broadway
Frederick Housman, 20 Broad Street
Francis M. Hugo, Secretary of State
August Janssen, Hof Brau House,
Broadway & 13th Street
Albert Keller, General Manager,
Ritz-Carlton Hotel
Henry Kelly Jr., 421 West 14th Street
Eroll Kerr, 347 Madison Avenue
David H. Knott, Sheriff, 35 Fifth Avenue
Jules C. LaVin, 1480 Broadway
C.R. MacDonald, 674 Hudson Street
Robert S. Maffitt, 1480 Broadway
Eugene D. Miller, Hotel Baltimore
George Pratt, Hotel Wolcott, West 49th Street
John Ringling, Ringling Brothers Circus,
Madison Square Gardens
Fred A Reed, Park Avenue Hotel
Thomas W. Rush, Surveyor, Port of New York
August Silz, 416 West 14th Street
E. M. Statler, Hotel Pennsylvania
George Sweeney, Hotel Commodore,
West 42nd Street
Edward M. Tierney, Hotel Ansonia
Oscar Tschirky, Waldorf Astoria
Senator James J. Walker, 6 St. Kukes Place

L.C. Wallick, 509 Times Building
James Woods, Hotel Belmont, West 42nd Street
Burton White, Hotel Bossert, Brooklyn
Alfred Cremona, Hotel Ambassador,
Atlantic City, New Jersey
George F. Parke, Florence Inn, Tarrytown,
New York
David B. Provan, Ritz-Carlton Hotel, Philadelphia

The Californians who will attend the party
include:

Charles Baad, Hotel Alexandria, Los Angeles
William F. Banks, Ambassador Hotel, Los Angeles
Vernon Goodwin, Mgt. Dir. of the Ambassador
System, Los Angeles
Thomas J. Coleman, St. Francis Hotel,
San Francisco
D.M. Linnard, Proprietor, Fairmont Hotel,
San Francisco
Roy L. Linnard, Fairmont Hotel, San Francisco
Halsey E. Manwaring, Palace Hotel, San Francisco
Alfred K. Bennett, The Ambassador,
Santa Barbara, California
Natt Head, Hotel Del Monte,
Del Monte, California
George O. Coulston, Pres.& G.M.,
California Hotel Co., Pasadena
Baron Long, U.S. Grand Hotel,
San Diego, California
W.A. Turquand, Hotel Del Coronado,
Coronado Beach
George O. Rolf, Hotel Utah, Salt Lake City, Utah
Sam Dutton, The Albany Hotel, Denver, Colorado

Calvin H. Morse, Brown Palace Hotel,
Denver, Colorado
John Burke, Congress Hotel, Chicago, Illinois
Tracy Drake, Blackstone Hotel, Chicago, Illinois
John D.Drake, Blackstone Hotel, Chicago, Illinois
Tom Taggart Jr., French Lick Springs Hotel, French
Lick, Indiana

While planning for his party, Penrose still had time to develop his 3,500-acre Turkey Creek ranch south of Colorado Springs, which was used to raise produce, vegetables and meat for the Broadmoor. "The finest Holstein bull ever brought into Colorado arrived on July 22 (1920) at the Turkey Creek ranch of Spencer Penrose," said a story in the *Denver Post* in announcing the acquisition by Penrose of the bovine aristocrat. Sir Pietertje Ormsby Fobes was a four-year-old senior grand champion at the Kansas City livestock show of the previous winter. He was purchased from Sam Carpenter, Oswego, Kansas, livestock breeder. Charles W. Wilson of Oswego, the new manager of the Penrose farm, negotiated the deal. The price was $15,000. Sir Pietertje, in the fashion of midwest oil millionaires, was to reproduce his kind among the Oswego herds in wintertime and spend summers in the Pikes Peak area.

Penrose made news wherever he went. Denver and Colorado Springs dailies reported on August 22, 1920, that clothes and jewelry valued at $1,000 belonging to Penrose's crony Clarence W. Hamlin, referred to as a Colorado Springs newspaper owner and politician, were stolen from Penrose's car while it was parked in front of a Welton Street restaurant. It was quite unlikely that Penrose and Hamlin were eating in that restaurant at the time. They were more likely to have been downing a few at the Denver Club, a three-story brownstone in downtown Denver.

One of Speck's favorite occupations at this time was shooting wildlife on the Great Plains east of Colorado Springs from a 1913 Pierce-Arrow touring car. And often he would start the day by mounting his horse and riding to the top of Cheyenne Mountain to see what he called "the most glorious vision nature had to offer — the sunrise."

There was nothing that more suited Speck's sense of the magnificence, his showmanship and flair for the unusual than the hotelmen's party, which he dubbed his "Arabian Nights Excursion." By now Colorado Springs was advertised as a "scenic wonderland and health resort," and the Broadmoor had become known as "the world's finest resort hotel complex" with 3,000 acres of Colorado showplace including a new eighteen hole golf course, glass enclosed pool for year-round swimming, riding stables with 135 stalls and the finest riding horses, and tours in easy range to Pikes Peak, Garden of the Gods, Cheyenne Mountain, Cripple Creek, Seven Falls, and the Springs at Manitou.

Speck was joined by Charles Tutt Jr. at the Santa Fe railroad station to greet his guests for the big bash. Everyone was lodged at "Speck's place," the palatial Broadmoor. Speck's friend Chester Arthur was there as well as Governor Shoup. For a special parade the governor dressed in chaps, bandanna, and sombrero. He had planned to ride a cow pony but could not find one to accommodate his rotundity. During their stay at the Broadmoor, the guests were entertained with every sort of sport, from polo and poker to automobile races up Colorado's most famous mountain and aeroplane races over its top. Entertainment also included dinner, dances, and elaborate parties. They visited Manitou, Cave of the Winds, and Williams Canyon, rode the railway to the top of Mt. Manitou, lunched at the Cliff House in Manitou

Springs, saw Glen Cove Inn, watched a polo game at Cheyenne Mountain Country Club, golfed at the Broadmoor Golf Club, and saw a performance in the "Little Theatre."

After the first night of the party, Speck routed out his astonished guests before daylight to show them the sunrise. As self-proclaimed "Super Chef of the World," Speck introduced the forty-one hotel barons to his "cooking club" that had cost him close to $500,000. Every known device for preparation of exotic dishes was available — ranges, grills, broilers, salamanders, ovens, iceboxes, deep-freezes, and expensive vintage wines ($25 wholesale) to wash the dishes down. After the soiree, one *Denver Post* article reported how famous Oscar had surrendered to Speck, whose culinary experience had been limited to "cooking up schemes for making money" as being a chef "without peer."

On the third day of festivities, the hotelmen finally settled down to some serious business. They discussed the merits of a hotel standardization scheme that would provide official classifications and ratings of hotels. They wanted to get back to the old rule of "pay for what you get and be sure you get what you pay for." Advocates of the system argued that both legitimate hotelmen and the public would benefit. The discussion continued during the short intervals between the entertainment arranged in their honor.

Finally, the hotelmen boarded the private railroad cars that would return them to their homes. Many were exhausted, some were still ready for more, but all were inspired by the magnificent setting and the untiring Penrose hospitality. Triumphantly, Speck stepped back into the shadows of Cheyenne Mountain and his beautiful Broadmoor, satisfied that he had successfully reciprocated the group who had so honored him.

CHAPTER XVIII

THE SMOKE-FILLED ROOM

S pencer Penrose, scion of an aristocratic Philadelphia family and born in the immediate post-Civil War period, could hardly be anything else politically but a Republican. He was big business, a hard money man who did not think that the working man who had dug his millions out of the ground for him should have higher wages or better working conditions.

If Speck needed an influence to strengthen his political faith, it was in the person of his older brother Boies Penrose, United States Senator from Pennsylvania. Senator Penrose — dissolute, arrogant, autocratic — served his political apprenticeship in both houses of the Pennsylvania legislature in Harrisburg, which were controlled by one of the most corrupt political machines of the time. He had served in the state house from 1884 to 1886 and had moved to the state senate in 1886, serving as president pro tem from 1889 to 1891. On January 27, 1897, he resigned the state legislature to enter the U.S. Senate.

Boies had not planned on the United States Senate but instead wanted to be mayor of Philadelphia where the swag was. Accordingly he was a candidate for mayor in 1895, being opposed for the Republican nomination by a "reform" candidate. But, as it turned out, State Senator Penrose was his own worst enemy. Now over 300 pounds, he not only developed a well-earned reputation as a glutton who was growing fatter and heavier after each voluminous meal he devoured, but bachelor Boies indulged himself in illegal activities at some of the city's better-known bordellos. While his supporters chuckled at his illicit antics, the opposition (headed up by John Wanamaker, merchant prince and former Postmaster General) put together a plan that became the big man's undoing — at least in this mayoralty race.

One morning, just before dawn, as Boies departed from one of Philadelphia's popular whore houses, a photographer stepped from the shadows with the explosion of his camera. Later a copy of the candid picture was presented to Boies, and he was told that if he did not withdraw his nomination for mayor, the photograph would be published in the daily newspaper the morning of the GOP Nominating Convention and end his political career once and for all. A bitter Boies Penrose reluctantly withdrew his nomination for mayor — the obesity people could take, but patronizing prostitutes would have blown his election sky high in the City of Brotherly Love where so many Puritan-like voters determined the outcome. However, this by no means ended his political life.

The ruling element of the party put Boies in the U.S. Senate two years after his ill-fated attempt at running for mayor of Philadelphia. This was not difficult inasmuch as legislatures at the time elected U.S. senators and this faction controlled the legislature. It was said that Speck's generous campaign contributions maintained the Senator as political dictator of Pennsylvania for almost two decades.

Boies Penrose, Speck's oldest brother, became a member of the Pennsylvania State Legislature after serving with a prominent Philadelphia law firm. Later, following an ill-fated attempt to run for mayor in the City of Brotherly Love, he was elected to the U.S. Senate where he became known as a strong man and kingmaker.
R.L. Olson Personal Collection

Boies aligned himself with the ultra-conservative reactionary faction of the GOP and in a short time became its leader. By 1912, his seniority had given him enough power when coupled with that of Senator Reed Smoot of Utah, he was able to force the party to renominate President William H. Taft, who carried only the small states of Vermont and Utah in the election.

While Speck waged big political bets and was known in the Rockies as a competent poker player, Boies never played cards. It is told, however, that he did play one game of poker on a train en route to a national convention. With customary beginner's luck, Boies stood several raises in a big pot. After asking what cards all one color meant, he raised out his opponents, threw down four hearts and one diamond, raked in the winnings, and never played again in his life.

Boies' popularity as a politician stretched all the way back to Colorado. At Fountain Valley Boys School in Colorado Springs, a portrait of the robust senator was hung in a prominent place — but only after a cigar in his right hand was painted out. Later, a Boies Penrose Memorial Hall was established where the cigarless portrait was placed.

Speck Penrose, still young looking and vigorous at fifty, became a delegate to the 1916 GOP National Convention. Speck got so carried away with the party's choice that he waged bets totaling $175,000 that the eminent jurist, Charles Evans Hughes, would beat the incumbent Democrat, Woodrow Wilson. America went to bed on election night in the belief that Hughes had been elected, the GOP having carried most of the large eastern states. Speck and his friends were so cock-sure of winning that they started a victory celebration about 8 p.m. on Tuesday, and the party continued through the night. With the dawn came the news that Wilson had carried the South, Ohio, and everything west of the Mississippi. He had been reelected. Speck had a $175,000 hangover.

But 1920 was another story. Boies Penrose was now in full command of the conservative majority of the Senate. Three months before the June 12 GOP National Convention in Chicago, Boies "selected" obedient, though colorless, Ohio Senator Warren G. Harding to be the GOP candidate for president. Boies picked Harding because he thought he could win. However, while grooming Senator Harding for the nomination, and after receiving less than favorable reports about a speech made by his candidate, Boies ordered Harding to make no more public addresses until after he was elected president. Unfortunately as the date of the convention neared, Penrose became seriously ill and was confined to his home in Philadelphia, forcing him to "run" it from his sick bed via a telephone hookup that cost him $800 a day.

At about midnight on the night before the convention, twelve trusted lieutenants of Senator Penrose gathered in a

While staying in Philadelphia in 1915, the Penroses had their portraits painted by English artist Julian Story. At the time Speck was fifty and Julie forty-five-years old. Nine years earlier the couple had been married in London. Well-known author Marshall Sprague noted in his book, Newport in the Rockies, that Speck's portrait "was too pretty, missing the Roman-gladiator beauty, quiet authority and bigness" which marked his appearance.

Courtesy, Special Collections, Tutt Library, Colorado College.

Chicago hotel room. The select group included Boies' old political partner, Senator Reed Smoot of Utah, Senators John T. King of Connecticut, James E. Watson of Indiana, James Wadsworth of New York, John W. Weeks of Michigan and Albert B. Fall of New Mexico; former Ohio Governor Willis; Senators Moses of New Hampshire, Harry R.New of Indiana; Harry Dougherty, the man chosen to be Harding's campaign manager; and Spencer Penrose. Speck was there not as a delegate but because he was the Senator's brother and because he was a very rich man who made a substantial campaign contribution of $175,000 to the 1920 campaign, no doubt in defiance of his lost bets during the 1916 election.

This was the infamous smoke-filled room where the leaders had gathered to ratify the choice of Senator Penrose back in Philadelphia. Democrats were quick to charge that Harding, who entered the convention with about forty votes and was looked upon merely as a favorite son, was "nominated" in a smoke-filled room by a mere handful of Boies Penrose's lackeys. Political writers and historians have made this "smoke-filled room" a historical term.

So the 1920 Republican National Convention was something of a Penrose convention with Speck permitted to sit in on the ratification of his brother's choice for president. So skillfully did Boies maneuver Harding's candidacy prior to and during the convention that the "dark horse" Ohioan was picked on the tenth ballot, while opposing candidates, led by popular Governor Calvin Coolidge of Massachusetts, were overwhelmingly defeated principally as a back-lash of the war with which the Wilson administration was saddled. The Democratic nominee was Governor James E. Cox, another Ohioan.

When Boies took his seat in the 60th Congress in January 1921, he was third in seniority. Working as chairman of the powerful Senate Finance Committee, handling tax and tariff legislation, was a greater hardship than he realized. Boies died in his Washington, D.C., home on December 31, 1921, one of the few men who had the personal satisfaction of knowing that he had hand-picked a man to run for the presidency, then manipulated him into the White House. When he died Boies was sixty-one, six feet four and one half inches tall, and weighed over 300 pounds. The Colorado press eulogized him with glowing editorials. The *Denver Post* said that Colorado had lost a good friend who made frequent trips to the state — he charmed people with his alluring personality and he was considered by all to be the most powerful figure in the U.S. Senate. His estate reportedly consisted of $250,000 in gold coin and stock in Speck's mining property.

Three years of the Harding "Ohio Gang" rule started with three of the men in the smoke-filled room gaining cabinet posts. This included Dougherty, Attorney General; Weeks, Secretary of War; and Fall, Secretary of Interior. The expose of the notorious "Teapot Dome" scandal (the famous oil swindle in Wyoming involving, among others, Speck's friends, Henry Blackmer and Verner Reed, as well as Interior Secretary Fall) ended with the sudden death of Harding while he toured the West Coast in 1923.

After serving less than a year as the appointed president, Calvin Coolidge was elected to that office in 1924. Four years later Speck bolted to the Al Smith camp since GOP candidate Herbert Hoover (a close personal friend of Dick Penrose) did not support repeal.

There is no record or recollection on any more large Penrose political bets until 1936 when Speck wagered $50,000 that Governor Alf Landon would lick Franklin D. Roosevelt. He did this knowing full well that Roosevelt was a shoo-in,

During the last year of President Warren G. Harding's administration, he was a guest at the Denver Press Club. Speck's oldest brother, Boies, had been instrumental in getting him elected. It was a great accomplishment although his administration was far from outstanding.

Denver Public Library Western Collection. F26353.

which turned out to be true with Landon carrying only two states, Maine and Vermont. But Speck was willing to pay the fifty grand just to show his contempt for Roosevelt and the New Deal, which replaced prohibition as his favorite hatred. Speck allowed the press to quote him as saying, "Roosevelt helped us replace prohibition, except for that I am against everything he ever did or ever will do."

One day during the New Deal era, while inspecting photographs of a pet building project, Speck was told that the two government-type workmen's outhouses in the foreground of the picture would be painted out. He protested indignantly, "Paint 'em out? Have you no soul? The government designed them and I dedicated them to President Roosevelt."

CHAPTER XIX

AT HOME
AND ABROAD

When good fortune began to smile on Speck Penrose in his Cripple Creek days, he thought he could see the fruition of his all-consuming ambition — to get rich, filthy rich, in the shortest possible time. He had attained this goal as early as the 1910-15 pre-income-tax period, but he kept building his interests in Colorado, Utah and other places in the American West.

In the early 1920s, Speck and Julie began living the good life on a grand scale. Speck's Republicans had taken over the country in 1921, thanks to Boies, so nothing remained for him on the political front except his running battle with prohibition.

In 1921, Penrose, who had long been Utah Copper Company's majority stockholder, dropped everything else long enough to negotiate the sale of the control of the firm to Kennecott. This was not a merger. Kennecott acquired control by purchase of Utah Copper stock. After the negotiation, Speck became the largest stockholder of the largest copper producer in the world — he made forty million dollars in profit. For fifteen years he had been placing some of his very substantial profits into the development of large copper properties including the Ray Consolidated Companies in Arizona and the Chino Mines of New Mexico. The gross value of production of Bingham Canyon from a modest 1903 beginning had reached the millions.

On May 16, 1921 Speck, who had been quoted as saying "no man is worth more than a dollar a day," sued the U.S. Government for a $12,538 rebate on his income tax. Just three months later, in this seemingly extreme step in another direction, he became a "wild one" in honor of the annual Colorado Springs roundup.

The following year, Speck's old Socialite drinking buddy and former Teller County District Attorney, Henry Blackmer, made international news when it was alleged that he was involved in the much-publicized Teapot Dome Scandal. To escape testifying, he fled to France where he became the world's most famous fugitive from justice.

In 1923, Charlie MacNeill died, first having frittered away his fortune on Wall Street, dropping eight million dollars in one day. This left Speck more bitter than before with "those Wall Street hibinders." They had taken away his drinking partner, long-time friend, founder of the Penrose Gold Mill trust, and co-developer of the Broadmoor — all of which meant a great deal to Speck.

On July 17, 1924, Speck announced his plans to build an eight-mile road up the face of Cheyenne Mountain. At the upper end would be an elaborate stone pavilion and dance floor with a panoramic view of the mountains and plains. It was to cost $350,000, and would incorporate his Cooking Club Road (up to the area where he practiced his new-found hobby), ending at the "Horns" — two gigantic boulders that hover above the plains at the southeast corner of the entrance.

Julie and Speck became extensive world travelers. When they returned from a European trip in 1924, Speck told the press, "The whole world, except France, has been humbugged by the Germans." Then he went on to tell how the rich Germans were outspending all others who traveled in Europe. But the Penroses lived like royalty, going abroad whenever the spirit moved them, and that was about once a year. Nothing was to interfere with their departure on an overseas tour, nor with the length of their stay, once they made up their minds to go.

Two instances bear this out. In 1924, Julie Penrose was a Colorado GOP presidential elector. The electors were to meet at the state capitol in Denver on January 12, 1925, to cast their ballots for Coolidge and Dawes. The Penroses threw a monkey wrench into the electoral machinery by announcing that they would depart for Europe on January 5. Couldn't they wait a week so everything would be legal? No! Finally a substitute was permitted to cast Julie's vote.

On February 27, 1925, while Julie and Speck leisurely toured the continent, Tal, who was traveling on a train from Aiken, South Carolina, to Philadelphia, suddenly keeled over and died. This untimely death was a shock to his survivors. Now, Speck and Dick were the only members of the family left. Dick, a mild-mannered, dignified, tolerant person, was the executor of his father's estate. On April 4, 1925, he cabled Speck in Paris that he had some very urgent family estate matters to discuss with him. When no reply came from Speck, Dick wrote him on April 25, quite impatiently saying that many things should be "acted upon by you and me or I must attend to these matters personally with no member of the family to consult." On May 27, Speck bought an elephant in Ceylon to be "golf caddy" at his Broadmoor golf course. When Speck finally returned to Colorado Springs in June, Dick berated him in somewhat strong terms for letting his own pleasure always take precedence over some of these important family matters.

Speck's actions indicated that he was somewhat indifferent to his brother's concern. One of the first things he did upon returning home was to buy the Pikes Peak cog railroad for $50,000. It had originally been built by the founder of the Simmons Mattress Company, the bed man. Later that month Speck launched what became an endless battle with the U.S. Internal Revenue. He filed suit in the U.S. District Court against the IRS for assessing him for $85,799 income tax.

By July the Penroses were again back on the continent. They maintained an apartment in Paris, bought a chateau in southern France, kept a house-boat on the Nile, and visited parts of Africa and Asia. Speck, now sixty, purchased a plantation in Hawaii and a home on the west coast. Then, of course, there was the old family house in Philadelphia, the Broadmoor, the El Pomar mansion, and the Turkey Creek ranch in Colorado.

When at his beloved Broadmoor, Speck was a super-showman. He lured celebrities to the appropriate place with a cameraman always on hand to get Speck's picture greeting them. Vice-president Dawes came, as did Shirley Temple. The humorist Will Rogers, whom Speck admired greatly, was a visitor. Speck rode forty miles on horseback to promote a wild west rodeo, straddled a trotting rig pulled by a llama in a parade, used an elephant as a caddy on his golf course, started the only mountainside zoo in the world, and conducted airplane races.

Speck had acquired one of the most complete collections of mammals, birds, reptiles, and amphibians in the country.

Speck gained visibility for his many causes by having his picture taken with the long list of celebrities and dignitaries who visited the Broadmoor. In 1925, he is shown here with Charles C. Dawes, on his right, vice president of the United States. Movie stars like Shirley Temple, sports figures such as Jack Dempsey, and, of course, his many friends like Will Rogers all had photographs taken with Speck.

Denver Public Library Western Collection. F13349.

Originally his zoo was next to the Broadmoor, but when a monkey bit a child and Speck was sued for $8,000 damages, he moved the zoo a mile and a half up Cheyenne Mountain. For the grand opening of the zoo, Speck hired a thirty-piece band from Ft. Logan, five army airplanes from Lowry Field, and the whole dedication was covered by Pathe Fox motion pictures for $500,000, plus related expenses.

Stories of Speck's elephants made wonderful newspaper copy, which Speck turned to his advantage for publicizing his Cheyenne Mountain Zoo. As one story goes, the maharajah of Nagapur, a graduate of Oxford and friend of the Penroses, heard that Speck had bought an elephant in Ceylon that died in Hamburg en route to the U.S. He made Speck a gift of the "Empress of India," a forty-five-year-old trained elephant. Back in Colorado Springs, the newspapers announced the newcomer, "For the first time, a palatial American resort hotel will have an elephant all its own for the pleasure of its guests, particularly children." Speck renamed her "Tessie" after the famous Cripple Creek whore, and with his friends, rode around the Broadmoor grounds on her back in a Hindu howdah. Speck loved Tessie and when she died of a heart attack ten years later he even planned to have her mounted — that is until he heard the price of taxidermy.

On January 24, 1926, while Speck and Julie were vacationing in Genoa, Italy, a notorious thief invaded their room in the Hotel Maramare. But, alas, this became the greatest mistake in the burglar's career. Sixty-year-old Speck caught him, beat him up single-handedly, and in the prowler's anxiety to escape he jumped out of a window twenty-four feet from the ground. Speck's friend Blackmer saw the whole thing and reported it to the Genoa newspapers that quickly hailed the rich American as a hero. The Italian press quoted Speck as saying, "I had a fine fight and came out with honors and a great deal of blood from the enemy. Henry M. Blackmer was on the floor above, and arrived just in time to see the burglar dive through the window. The robber left his sweater in my hands and so I have a souvenir of my visit in Italy. I was sixty years old last November second and I found I could fight just as well as when I was thirty down in Mexico. This makes me feel pretty young again."

In 1926, world heavyweight champion Jack Dempsey accepted an invitation from Penrose to train for his first Tunney fight at the Broadmoor. Jack had been introduced to Penrose at Cripple Creek in 1915, when Jack fought and barely defeated George Coplen, the mining town's white hope. When Jack arrived with his trainer, they were photographed with Mr. and Mrs. Penrose. Then for succeeding days Dempsey was put on exhibition, doing training stunts of various forms in the public view, always with a crowd on hand, trumped up by Speck's publicity man. The pressure of the Penrose-sponsored promotion activity became too much of a strain and distraction. Finally, Dempsey had to take off for Chicago in order to get in some serious training. This was the last time Dempsey recalls seeing Speck, just before his first defeat by Gene Tunney on September 23, 1926, in Philadelphia, before a record crowd of 120,000. A year later Tunney again defeated Dempsey in the battle of the "long count."

As indicated by his actions in Italy, Speck didn't know the meaning of physical fear. He abominated hypocrisy as the most cardinal sin, couldn't stand chamber music, and was a penny pincher who spent millions thinking nothing of it. Once while Julie was selecting art objects and furniture for the Broadmoor in Hong Kong, she chose some Peking Ming statuary that cost $15,000. When Speck saw she was particularly pleased with this, he said "send a dozen!" Yet, after a Utah Copper board meeting where hundreds of thousands were being negotiated, Speck saw an exact item in a window for forty-five cents that he had bought in another store for eighty-five cents. He angrily declared, "I'm going back to General Hardware and throw this through their God-damned window."

Speck kept a pad and pencil by his bed to jot down notions during the night. One year, in mid-January, he decided to have a watermelon party. The melons were kept cold by a mechanical icebox that he built before the days of refrigeration. At a cost of ten dollars each, Speck served all his guests cold watermelon.

One of Speck's pet peeves was personal publicity, particularly where he was described as a civic benefactor. Along with MacNeill and Hamlin, Speck bought the *Colorado Springs Telegraph*. The next morning Speck walked into the city room and announced, "the next S.O.B. that prints my name in this sheet is fired!" When MacNeill died he willed his share to Hamlin who thought it a good joke to resume the "multi-millionaire public benefactor" articles. It took months of Speck's fuming and ranting before Hamlin stopped, and Speck's name was finally handled as straight news.

But, everything Speck touched turned out to be news. Prowlers were driven from El Pomar on April 26, 1926, by shrieks of a specially-built siren and the employees, including guards equipped with an arsenal of ammunition, revolvers and two Browning machine guns. Speck offered a $1,000 reward to any of his employees who would shoot dead an intruder.

Speck bought the Manitou Water Company in October of 1926 and immediately launched a nation-wide advertising campaign promoting the district, its mineral waters, his bottling works, and warehouse. He also bought the first Colorado Capitol Building where the second territorial legislature met in 1862. He had it moved from Colorado City, where it had housed a Chinese laundry, and placed it on the Broadmoor property as a tourist attraction.

That same year Speck auctioned off 100 thoroughbred cattle to make way for blooded horses from a Kentucky Derby winning stable, making Colorado Springs the horse breeding and equestrian sport center of the entire West. Later, Speck offered his luxurious El Pomar mansion to President Coolidge for the 1927 summer White House.

Speck, who had a special liking for the "Old West" with its rodeos, cowboys, and Indians, introduced the rodeo to the Broadmoor in 1927. He first named his rodeo after Will Rogers. Later, it became known as the Penrose Stadium Rodeo, and eventually the annual "Pikes Peak or Bust Rodeo." The stadium provided 10,000 covered seats. Often Speck allowed Indians to set up their tepees on the Broadmoor grounds; and in 1927, he was made a chief of the Sioux tribe in a special ceremony complete with buffalo-horned headdress, moccasins, and war paint. Speck commissioned Maxfield Parrish to paint a picture of his Broadmoor, thereby proclaiming the beauty of the scene to the world and using it to exploit his pet project. This painting, one of the artist's most widely known works, has helped make the Broadmoor known throughout the world.

While traveling in France in 1927, Speck's left eye became seriously infected, necessitating its removal by Paris specialists. From that time on, Penrose had a glass eye. This was the eye he had injured in 1883, after which he could do very little reading. At a later date it was revealed that in order to match his right eye, weathered by so many years of carousing, long nights, and heavy drinking, his glass eye had been carefully designed to look bloodshot.

CHAPTER XX

LAST OF
THE PENROSES

Spencer and Julie Penrose were honored guests at the unveiling of a statue of Speck's older brother, the late United States Senator Boies Penrose, on the capitol grounds in Harrisburg, Pennsylvania, on September 23, 1930. The only other living Penrose brother, R.A.F. (Dick) Penrose Jr., was also a special guest. An invitation to each brother was extended by Governor John S. Fisher of the Keystone state.

At the ceremonies, due respect was paid to the senator who "for many years represented Pennsylvania in the upper house of Congress and was one of the outstanding national leaders of the Republican party."

When Speck returned from Pennsylvania, he planned a trip to lower California to start construction of a bungalow at a new resort which was being developed there. Speck planned to occupy the new place the following spring after his return from a trip to Europe where he and Julie would spend the 1930-31 winter.

On July 30, 1931, Dick Penrose passed away in Philadelphia. This made Speck the last of the Penroses. Dick's obituary in the *Denver Post* paid him an appropriate tribute.

Richard A.F. Penrose, prominent mining engineer and geologist of Philadelphia, and only remaining brother of Spencer Penrose of Colorado Springs,
died in his home city Thursday night, according to
information received by the Colorado Springs millionaire at his home, El Pomar, in Broadmoor.

Richard Penrose was a bachelor, and his only
surviving relative is Spencer Penrose.

Mr. and Mrs. Penrose left today to attend the
funeral in Philadelphia, which, following the custom of the Penrose family for many years, will be
strictly private.

Richard Alexander Fullerton Penrose was born
in 1863, the son of Richard Alexander Fullerton
Penrose, a noted physician of Philadelphia, and
Sarah Hannah Boies Penrose.

He was graduated from Harvard University
as a geologist and engineer and became nationally
prominent in his profession as a lecturer, writer,
associate editor of scientific journals and in practical geology surveys for various states and for the
United States geological survey.

He was an authority on the iron and mag-
nesium ores of Arkansas and mineral deposits of
Texas, on which his official reports were adopted
as outstanding authorities. He spent months on the
geology of the Cripple Creek district on behalf of
the United States geological survey and his books
on the gold camp are among those of the highest
authorities.

Dick Penrose, as he was popularly known in his
profession, was lecturer on geology at Stanford University for several years and gave lectures on the same
subject at Harvard and other universities. He traveled

extensively in Siberia and wrote a book, *The Last Stand of Old Siberia*, which predicted the inroads of the Russian government that have now taken place. He was the author of numerous books, one of the latest being *What the Engineer Can Do in War*.

Dr. Charles B. Penrose of Philadelphia, an older brother of Spencer Penrose, died in his native city February 28, 1925, and the United States Senator Boies Penrose died in Washington, D. C. January 1, 1922.

Dick was the "different" Penrose — brilliant geologist and mining engineer, modest, quiet in manner and mode of living, serious minded, a two-drink-per-day man (Boies would down a quart of bourbon with his gargantuan meal) and, like Boies, a bachelor. His passing was keenly felt by Speck who recalled that it was Dick of all the brothers who manifested the greatest interest in Speck's success at the time the latter was in New Mexico and trying to get going on a career; and it was Dick's professional counsel that led Spencer to his gold and copper fortunes. Conversely, Speck helped Dick in no small way. Dick left a fortune of $10,000,000, most of it derived from investments in Speck's mining ventures. Dick's will provided that his personally acquired fortune be divided equally between the Geological Society of America and the American Philosophical Society. In 1927, several years before Dick's death, the Geological Society of America established the Penrose Medal award, given annually to individuals who made outstanding contributions to the geological sciences. Today it is recognized as the most prestigious award given in the field of earth sciences.

Speck was the only remaining Penrose. His younger brothers, Phillip and Francis (Friday) Penrose had died due to ill health in their early twenties. As the obituary said, Boies passed away in 1921 and Tal died in 1925.

In the same fateful year of the death of Dick Penrose (1931), at a time when Speck boasted of robust good health at sixty-six, he was threatened briefly with cancer, causing him to begin thinking about what to do with his fabulous fortune and planning his final resting place.

After four decades of happiness at the foot of Pikes Peak, Speck did not wish to end up among the stuffy Penrose blue bloods in Philadelphia's Laurel Hill Cemetery. He hired an architect to plan a memorial tower several hundred feet high, located about three miles from the top of Cheyenne Mountain. The magnificent granite tower was built with a circular staircase leading to a balcony that commanded a startling view for miles, the center of which was Speck's Broadmoor empire.

Speck was dissuaded by friends from calling the structure the Penrose Memorial. As he pondered his next move, his good friend Will Rogers was killed in an airplane crash near Point Barrow, Alaska. With Rogers' death, a great wave of sentiment swept over the whole country and many structures were named for him. Speck decided then and there to call his memorial "The Will Rogers Shrine of the Sun." He hired sculptor Jo Davidson to carve the figure and face of America's number one humorist and philosopher. The area around the shrine had been incorporated as a cemetery called "End of the Trail Association."

Later, frescoes were painted on the interior walls by Randall Davey of Santa Fe, depicting phases of life in the Pikes Peak region. These featured Speck Penrose from the earliest days, the discovery of gold by Womack, the interior of a saloon, dance hall and gambling establishment, and the

Will Rogers was one of the country's most popular comedians and philosophers during the early part of the last century and his image lives on today. Speck's old acquaintance was a familiar sight at the Broadmoor Hotel where his laid-back and spontaneous sense of humor charmed everyone. His tragic and fatal airplane crash in Alaska was a shock to the whole nation and one that was felt around the world. It was a fitting tribute to Will Rogers to memorialize his life at the Shrine of the Sun above the Broadmoor.
Denver Public Library. 22163.

exterior of the frame shack occupied by Penrose with boom-day scenes in the background. At the dedication, there was a polo tournament, rodeo, and other events favored by Rogers. A sodium flare was lit on the pinnacle of the shrine to burn forever, and chimes were installed to ring out every fifteen minutes. Floodlights made the shrine visible 100 miles across the eastern plains.

Speck's many financial and business successes had given him a buoyant optimism. In April of 1931, Speck and Julie returned from another tour of Europe. In an interview he said that on his stopover in New York he found much evidence that prosperity would soon return to the country. He backed his confidence in an economic up-swing by announcing that he would launch a big building program at the Broadmoor. He went on to say "people in Europe seem to enjoy life more than we do. They have more leisure time and there is less crime in continental European countries than in the United States." He issued a similar statement in an interview given on September 3, 1931. But the depression was gradually tightening its grip, and Speck turned out to be a false prophet. He then made plans to leave in November for another winter in Paris.

When not abroad, the Penroses could be seen regularly around the Colorado Springs area in their 1928 V-8 Cadillac, specially made by Hibbard & Darrin in Paris. Actually it was Julie's car, inasmuch as her initials, JVLP (Julie Valliers Lewis Penrose), were tastefully placed on both front doors.

Over the years Speck became well known for his benevolence, eccentricities, and strong beliefs. He decided that he would turn his famous Pikes Peak highway over to the U.S. Government by 1935. Operated as a toll road for years, the "ladder to the sky," as he called it, extended 14,106 feet up to the very top and provided the setting for annual auto races.

Speck had gained the reputation as the "state's most assiduous wild animal shopper," as he collected for "the world's most elaborate zoo." He bought a pair of African lions from a noted big game hunter in Africa and bought another jungle king from a street carnival that played in Colorado Springs.

Although Speck was a member of more than twenty-four clubs, including the most exclusive in Paris, New York, and Philadelphia, his favorite was the Cooking Club in Colorado Springs. Its aim was "conviviality" and, according to Speck, the last member to go under the table was president. He had been president since its organization.

Everything Speck did was on a grand scale. Just prior to the opening of his new riding academy, Speck purchased an old bar mirror from pre-prohibition days and placed it at one end. Considered one of the finest riding academies in the country, the structure measured 100 by 300 feet without one pillar supporting the huge dome.

In the spring of 1932, sixty-six-year-old Speck observed the political scene. He watched the Republicans renominate President Hoover and fail to go on record for prohibition repeal. Having bolted the GOP to support Alfred E. Smith in 1928, he should have been overjoyed when the Democrats, at their Chicago convention, declared support for outright repeal. But, the Democrats also nominated Speck's fellow Harvard alum, Franklin D. Roosevelt, for president. It then became a case of which Penrose disliked the most — prohibition or F.D.R. In 1932, everyone knew that the Democrats would win easily, just as they knew that in 1920 the Republicans would win. Speck reasoned that the Democrats would repeal prohibition anyway; therefore, he could in good conscience support "Dry Hoover," which he did.

In 1949 Henry H. Blackmer, on the left, returned to Colorado after twenty-five years of self-imposed exile. He had been accused by the United States government of playing a part in the beleaguered Tea Pot Dome scandal. Blackmer had been one of the original members of the Socialites in Cripple Creek and one of Speck's good friends. Speck supported Blackmer from the very first accusation. Denver Public Library Western Collection.

Every chance Speck got he defended his friend Henry Blackmer, the self-exiled magnate caught up in the Teapot Dome scandal. Speck branded the senatorial oil investigation as "political propaganda," and said that Blackmer would return to the U.S. "when he's ready."

Interestingly enough, when news of Speck's Paris eye operation reached the press in Colorado, Speck recounted a "yacht race" off Long Island as the original cause of his lost eye — not while he was trying out for the Crimson crew at Harvard.

The older Speck got, the more he philosophized. "Any man who works after noon is a damned fool" was a favorite statement of Speck's. "Don't sell the U.S. short," Speck said about the depression. "Great fortunes were evolved from the panic of 1893, particularly in the West — and history will probably repeat itself." Then with another deep puff on his cigar he concluded, "The entire country is on the upgrade and as the wheel turns, prosperity will come back and we will get over our scare."

CHAPTER XXI

A GREAT PHILANTHROPY

About the time in 1931, when it was feared that Speck had cancer, the *Denver Post* printed a story that pictured the multi-millionaire tycoon in robust health. Sixty-five-year-old Penrose, the yarn recounted, arose each morning shortly after six and by 6:45 was walking briskly around the private lake at his El Pomar estate attired in a bathing suit with Julie and their English sheep dogs at his side. This signaled the approach of the feeding hour for some 200 ducks, swans, and geese.

By this time, Speck had stopped acquiring mining properties and with Julie was living a relaxed life in the Pikes Peak area or abroad. Once the prohibition law was repealed on December 5, 1933, one of Speck's greatest campaigns finally came to an end, and he could concentrate on community and Broadmoor promotions.

In 1935, Speck declared publicly that he wanted to be the Republican leader of Colorado. He was confident that he could put the broken pieces together and rehabilitate the party, now in despair because of complete Democratic control of the state and nation. Roosevelt's New Deal became

The raised eyebrow, mustache and wide-brimmed hat were well know traits of Spencer Penrose. The familiar look was embellished in this photograph taken at the Berkeley Lainson studio, for many years a fixture at the Brown Palace Hotel in Denver. Circa 1935.

Courtesy, Berkeley Lainson.

Speck's most popular target for criticism. His political interest, however, did not deter Speck from philanthropic and other projects.

In 1936, Speck sponsored the Denver-to-Pikes-Peak air races, and later he formally and proudly presented the U.S. Government with the Pikes Peak Highway that he had built twenty years before. Despite his poor health in 1937, Speck's physical activities continued to be a topic of conversation. He swam and rode daily, and in some circles was still considered a skilled boxer.

As early as 1931 when Speck had his health scare, he began seriously studying the eventual disposal of his vast wealth. He conferred frequently with his Denver attorney, Henry McAllister, and with financiers and bankers. One matter that troubled him and increased his determination to set up some sort of tax free philanthropy was the precipitous increase in federal taxes, particularly on the wealthy, that was being used to finance the New Deal agencies now attempting to lift the nation out of the economic depression.

In December 1937, Spencer Penrose climaxed his great and spectacular career with the incorporation of the El Pomar Foundation "exclusively for charitable uses and purposes as well, in the absolute and uncontrollable discretion of the trustees, most effectively to assist, encourage, and promote the general well being of the inhabitants of the state of Colorado and the principal and income from its funds and property shall be limited for use within the state of Colorado."

Trustees of the foundation were Charles L. Tutt Jr., William L. Howbert, M.W. Bogart, and Henry McAllister. Into this foundation Speck transferred all of his copper assets and his Pikes Peak properties valued at many millions. The copper stock would earn two to three million dollars a year for

Speck, Julie and their dog stroll through the Italian Garden behind El Pomar. Speck was apparently a hands-on owner who had regular consultations with the gardeners. Circa 1937.

Denver Public Library Western Collection. F13347.

the foundation, but the Broadmoor Hotel proved to be a money loser. It had cost Speck from $50,000 to $150,000 a year in operating losses since 1918. Speck never made a dime on the Broadmoor because he allowed it to be turned into a nest of thieves, moochers, spongers, and incompetents. At one time he had 100 employees and two guests.

During the depression the Broadmoor hung on, although services were cut and unused wings were closed. One of the highlights during this lull was an all-night party given by the Junior League in 1933, which included a dinner dance, a parade of 300 animals around the lake, and a frolic in the lake 'til pre-dawn.

The Broadmoor was closed the winter of 1935 and not reopened until June 1, 1936. Before the end of the year, the Tavern off the front lobby became a focal point of the hotel, featuring dining in an atmosphere of empty bottles from Speck's wine cellar.

In 1938, after a cruise of Europe, Speck completed the last of many, many physical attractions at the Broadmoor — the Penrose Stadium, across the lake from the hotel. This stadium became the home of the annual Colorado Springs "Pikes Peak or Bust" rodeo. The Broadmoor already had two 18 hole golf courses, stables, seven separate dining and drinking spots within the complex, garage facilities, a museum, bowling lanes, a built-in movie theatre, a skeet range, and a host of elite shops. In August of 1938, Speck transferred ownership of his Cheyenne Mountain Zoo to the city of Colorado Springs.

Shortly thereafter, Speck developed a distressing throat ailment. The diagnosis was cancer. On June 23, 1939, Julie's granddaughter, the Baroness Pauline Longchamps of Belgium, and her children paid the Penroses a visit at El Pomar. In

September Speck's Colorado Springs physician, Dr. McCrossin, took him to Chicago where an operation failed to bring a favorable result. Speck, knowing that he had not long to live, took the news with his usual composure and returned to his beloved Pikes Peak domain. On December 7, 1939, just a month after he turned seventy-four, Speck passed away. He died in his room at El Pomar in front of the very large picture window overlooking his cherished Cheyenne Mountain. Speck's sole survivors were Julie and his step-daughter, Gladys, the Countess Cornet de Ways Ruart of Brussels, and her daughter.

"World-renowned Magnate and Resort Operator Dies at Colorado Springs Home" read the banner headline over accounts of Speck's life, which often filled a full page that ran in newspapers across the nation. Although he was called a cynic, dreamer and sentimentalist, his obituaries all paid tribute to the saga of his life. He was honored by Colorado Springs and mourned by literally millions who had known him or simply knew of him.

A complete atheist, Speck had always planned to be cremated, but he knew this would be opposed by Julie. He had made arrangements for his body to be whisked away after his death to the Fairmount Crematorium in Denver before Julie could compose herself and make arrangements according to her Catholic upbringing.

The secular funeral was held at the Shrine of the Sun with fewer than 100 in attendance, by invitation only. This included relatives (mostly Julie's side since Speck had none to invite) and close friends. Dixie McCrossin, the wife of Speck's doctor, carried Speck's ashes in a plain urn with a white gardenia on top while "Home on the Range" was sung. Henry McAllister, Speck's good friend and attorney, spoke

The Will Rogers Shrine of the Sun provides a magnificent panoramic view of Colorado's Front Range, looking east from the Rocky Mountains. It was built by Speck on his beloved Cheyenne Mountain for his final resting place. At about this time his friend, the internationally known philosopher and comedian, Will Rogers, was killed in an Alaskan plane crash. As a fitting tribute to his friend, Speck named the shrine in Will Roger's honor. In 1939, Speck's ashes were interred in the Shrine as were Julie's remains in 1956.

Denver Public Library. 14639

Colorado Historical Society

This Associated Press Wirephoto released at the time of Julie Penrose's death in January of 1956, shows her with her pet, Peti Pat. Julie was described as Pikes Peak's leading benefactor. She died of cancer, just as Speck had. After a funeral at the Pauline Chapel, she was laid to rest next to her husband in the Will Rogers Shrine of the Sun.

Courtesy, Colorado Historical Society 86.296.073

briefly of the life that had come to an end. Although it was not a religious ceremony, Monsignor Kelly, Julie's close friend, gave the eulogy. The following day, the Shrine of the Sun was open for the general public to pay their last respects.

Under the floor of the very small chapel in the tower of the Shrine of the Sun, Spencer Penrose's ashes lie along with the first two friends he made in Cripple Creek — Harry Leonard and Horace Devereux. Harry Leonard had lived in Denver along with other prominent friends of Speck's, William Kistler, Claude Boettcher, and Charles Hughes. Horace Devereux lived in the Broadmoor the last few years of Speck's life, from '37 to '39. He had no money. Julie is there too, having died on January 23, 1956, at eighty-six. A Catholic, she was not cremated and was interred in an elegant bronze casket.

Years after Speck's death, historians recount the almost forgotten gold camp days of the Colorado Rockies. Over $770 million in gold ore had been taken from Teller County from 1891 to 1962, when the last mine was closed. Colorado mining camps made millionaires — H.A.W. Tabor, Moffatt, MacNeill — who all ultimately went broke. Spencer Penrose was one of few to not only keep what he made in mining but also add to it. Penrose was an investment genius with a touch of Barnum bally hoo. It took a daring, two-fisted explosive man to buck up against rough and tumble gold camps, gamble on copper ore mining and milling, and to enter a community not readily willing to accept outsiders.

In a booklet put out by the Central City Opera House where some chairs were dedicated to him, a brief biography of Speck said, "...broad, genial and loyal in his friendships, he always takes with a smile the criticisms and financial disappointments incidental to such vast enterprises and continues his unfailing and arduous work to make Colorado famous."

Some called Penrose a dreamer who put up a front of cynicism, but all agreed that he had a fantastic sense of humor. His whiplash sarcasm, keen cold intellect, and valiant willingness to take a chance, turned out to be a formula for success. He was the number one cutup, showpiece, magnifico, and public benefactor of his era. His rakish expression of one eyebrow lifted and the other lowered accentuated his self-assertive masculinity. He was, in two words of the times, a "swashbuckling grandee."

What could be the best monument to this man? Perhaps it could be Kennecott Copper — one of the world's greatest producers of copper, representing the largest individual movement of material of any kind made by man in world history. Or it could be the fabulous Broadmoor — one of the most luxurious resort hotels of the day. Or, perhaps, it might be the statue of Penrose, at the entrance to the El Pomar executive offices in the Broadmoor, complete with riding habit and wide brimmed hat, fittingly, made of copper. Or it possibly might be his bust in the Founders' Hall of the "National Cowboy Hall of Fame" in Oklahoma City.

When his estate was finally established, it was the largest sum ever filed for probate in the Rocky Mountain region. The assets of El Pomar have increased in value — from $17,000,000 in 1939, to more than $600,000,000 today — placing it high among the world's charitable trusts.

But no tribute would have been more appreciated by Speck than the yearly cocktail party given in his honor by his friends at the El Paso Club starting in 1939, using funds set aside for this purpose in his will by the man himself.

🖾 *The End* 🖾

EPILOGUE

After Speck's death, Julie gave up her personal maid, Ann, and moved from El Pomar into a seventh floor apartment in the Broadmoor. She was dubbed the dowager queen of Colorado Springs society. Surrounding herself with church people, she went to Mass almost daily. El Pomar was turned over to the Catholic Sisters of Charity of Cincinnati for a retreat house — the same order that operated Glockner Sanitorium.

Julie left a portion of her personal belongings in the thirty-room mansion. Some of the larger sitting rooms were converted into cubicles for the sisters. After every Mass at the El Pomar Retreat, a special prayer was said: "We beseech thee, O Lord, according to thy loving kindness, have mercy upon the soul of thy handmaiden, Julie Penrose."

As mentioned, Julie's miraculous return to Catholicism was a result of her devotion to Pauline, her granddaughter. It is said that reports came from Belgium about Pauline's illness. Wrought with emotion, Julie dramatically announced that if Pauline could only get well, she would return to the Church. When Pauline recovered, Julie not only returned to the religion in which she was raised, but behind the Broadmoor she built a replica of the private chapel of Pope Paul

III in Rome, and named it after her granddaughter. In 1942, Julie received the Papal Cross from Pope Pius XII for her generosity and loyalty.

A few years after Speck's death, Julie also bequeathed the Penrose Cancer Clinic to the Glockner Sanitorium. Originally opened in 1889, the Sanatorium had twenty-five beds. Three years later it was put into the hands of the Sisters of Charity of Cincinnati. Because of repeated donations from the Penroses, in 1947 its name was changed to Glockner-Penrose Hospital. In 1952, at the suggestion of its original founder, Mrs. Marie Glockner, the newly expanded 342-bed facility's name was changed again to Penrose Hospital.

Later in life, Julie's interest in the Broadmoor waned. Her attention turned to the zoo, Fountain Valley School, Central City Opera, and the Penrose Hospital. Additions to the hospital, sometimes referred to as the "Penrose Hilton" because of its ultra modern facilities, were continually built on to the complex. One of the last was an eleven-story, ten million dollar research building added in 1967. As president of the El Pomar Foundation, Julie oversaw the annual giving of about one million dollars annually to the Symphony, Pauline Memorial School, St. Mary's High School, Colorado Springs Fine Arts Center, and various nursing homes and youth organizations in Colorado Springs. She was also vice president of the Broadmoor Hotel Company, Chairman of the Board of the Central City (Colorado) Opera House, Cheyenne Mountain Museum, Zoological Society, and princess of many Western Indian tribes.

Two weeks after Speck's death, Charles Tutt Jr., the son of Speck's former partner, was named president of the Broadmoor Hotel Company, and he remained Julie's chief advisor until her death. Charles and his first wife Eleanor had three sons and a daughter — Charles Leaming Tutt III, who became Dean of General Motors Institute for Executives; William Thayer Tutt, who was the eventual president of the Boadmoor; Russell Thayer Tutt, who was a Director of El Pomar, vice president of the Broadmoor, and Chairman of the Board of Trustees of Colorado College in Colorado Springs; and Mrs. Joseph T. Mills (Josephine Thayer Tutt) of Rancho Santa Fe, California. After the death of his first wife, Charles married Vesta Wood and they had one son, John Wood Tutt. Charles Tutt Jr. died at age seventy-two on November 1, 1961. The El Pomar Foundation, of which Julie was president until her death, presented Colorado College with the Charles L. Tutt library in his honor.

After Speck's death, the Broadmoor moved into the black for the first time. There were almost 900 employees, twenty-five major buildings on 3,000 acres of land. Some of the old-timers hired by Speck included Louis Stratta, executive chief since 1918; Joseph "Jumbo" Flynn, a maitre d'; and William B. Hall, an early executive of the Broadmoor Hotel Company.

The new ten million dollar Broadmoor South nine-story wing added in 1960, increased the number of guest rooms to 145. The $2.5 million International Convention Center — which enclosed a hyperbolic paraboloid and could serve over 2,000 at once — made it ideal for the Broadmoor to host over 300 conventions and conferences attended by 50,000 in one year. Many of these were booked five or six, even fifteen, years in advance. The 1949 Governors' Convention was booked at the "world's most noted hotel." Later, a replica of a 19th century English pub, The Golden Bee, was added underneath the Convention Center.

Some of the special Broadmoor guests included well-known personalities of the day, such as Jeannette

MacDonald, James Milton, Paul Robeson, Tyrone Power, Gene Autry, Rudy Vallee, Hoagy Carmichael, Mickey Rooney, Carmen Miranda, Edgar Bergen, Clark Gable, King Hussein of Jordon, the Prince of Iraq, President Gronchi of Italy, Archduke Otto of Austria, the Maharajah of India, the King of Siam, General Eisenhower, Richard Nixon, Wendell Wilkie, Franklin D. Roosevelt, Herbert Hoover, Clare Booth Luce, Igor Stravinski, Edna Ferber, Truman Capote, Shirley Temple and, of course, Jack Dempsey.

In 1954, Julie built a striking guest house on Cheyenne Mountain — not far from the zoo — which she called her "shack." She spent $178,000 for the privilege of getting away from the hotel two or three times a year for small dinners. Besides the zoological haven for exotic animals, 9,565-foot Cheyenne Mountain was also a mecca for rest and sports, a grazing ground for prized beef, the heart of air-space defense for 220 million people of our nation at NORAD, and, of course, Speck's shrine. In 1942, over 35,000 military personnel were moved into Camp Carson, south of Colorado Springs; and in the late fifties, the U.S. Air Force Academy was established north of the city.

With her pet poodles, Peti Pat and Minion, Julie indulged herself in the arts. She loved opera, owned an original Picasso and bought a cottage in Central City, the silver mining community near Denver that since has become a tourist attraction. The "Spencer Penrose Music Award" that Julie established is still given each year to the outstanding high school musician in the Rocky Mountain region.

One day Julie and her chauffeur, Frosty, stopped by the Karabin house, a short distance from the Broadmoor. John Karabin was her doctor and Jean, his wife, had become a friend of Julie's. Behind the house near the stable, Julie spotted Jan Karabin, the doctor's teen-age daughter, crying because she had lost her horse. Without visiting with Jean, Julie left immediately. Before the end of the day a beautiful riding horse was delivered to the Karabin home without a word from its donor.

On January 23, 1956, eighty-five-year-old Julie died of the same disease that had taken her husband, cancer. At her bedside was her sister, Mrs. W. Howie Muir; her niece, Countess Cyril Tolstoi; Monsignor William Kelly; Charles L. Tutt Jr.; Robert V. Menary; Roland W. Giggey, her secretary; Dr. W.P. McCrossin; Paul Baschleben, her chauffeur; Hermine Weber, her male assistant; Dr. J.L. McDonald; Dr. Willard Smith; and four Catholic nuns.

Besides her sister Mrs. Muir and Julie's niece, who were with her at the time of her death, Julie was survived by her daughter Gladys, her other sister Mrs. Cameron Currie, her nephew John D. Currie, and six great-grand-children living in Belgium and Italy. Pauline, her beloved granddaughter, had died of a brain tumor in 1951. Julie's daughter Gladys, Countess Cornet de Ways Ruart, who had been stricken with multiple sclerosis, died on April 30, 1967.

Not long after Julie's remains were laid to rest along with Speck's at the Shrine of the Sun, Colorado historian Marshall Sprague said that Julie was "a phenomenally wonderful, generous, and stimulating person." Perhaps this is a fitting epitaph for the woman who spent over half of her life with one of the last great giants of the Old West.

BIBLIOGRAPHY

Books:

Bebe, Lucius. *The Big Spenders.* Doubleday & Co., Garden City, N.Y., 1966.

Bowden, Robert C. Boies Penrose — *Symbol of an Era.* Greenberg, 1937.

Davenport, Walter. *Boies Penrose.*

Fairbanks, Helen R. and Berkey, Charles R. *Life and Letters of R.A.F. Penrose. Jr..* The Geological Society of America, N.Y.C., 1952.

Hall, Francesca Tudor. *Colorado Springs Fifty Years Ago.* 1937.

Hammon, John H. *The Porphyry Coppers.* Washington, D.C. January, 1933.

Jackson, Wm. S. *Count Pourtales — Fifteen Western Years.* 1949.

Lee, Mabel Barbee. *Cripple Creek Days.* Doubleday & Co., Garden City, N.Y., 1958. *Back in Cripple Creek.* Doubleday & Co., 1968.

Ormes, Manly Dayton and Ormes, Eleanor. *The Book of Colorado Springs.* 1933.

Rogers, H.S. and McIntyre, W.H. *Colorado Springs. Colorado*

Sprague, Marshall. *Newport in the Rockies.* Sage Books, Denver, Colo., 1961.
Money Mountain: the Story of Cripple Creek Gold. Little Brown & Co., Boston, 1953.

Walters, Frank. *Midas of the Rockies* Sage Books, 1937.
Clarence Darrow for the Defense.
The Guggenheims.

Articles:

Central City Opera House Assn."The Glory That was Gold," Supplement to the 3rd Edition, 1937.

Ferrill, Will C."Sketches of Colorado," *Denver*, Western Press, 1911.

Press Biographies, "Representative Men of America," *Colorado Number*, July, 1906. -

Sprague, Marshall. "Good-bye Little London," *Colorado Magazine*, Denver, Summer, 1965."That Fabulous Broadmoor," *Denver Post* Empire Magazine, Denver, March 11, 1953. "Mr. Broadmoor," *Denver Post* Empire Magazine, February, 1953.

Stone, Wilbur F. "History of Colorado." Vol. Ill, *Chicago*, Clarke, 1918.

Wood, Nancy."The Broadmoor," *Colorado Magazine*, Denver, Spring, 1968.

Newspapers:

Colorado Springs Free Press
Colorado Springs Gazette
Colorado Springs Telegraph
Cripple Creek Crusher
Cripple Creek Gold Rush
Cripple Creek Mail
Cripple Creek Times
Denver Post
Rocky Mountain News

Pamphlets:

Bancroft, Caroline. *Six Racy Madams.* Johnson Publishing Co., Boulder, 1965.

Bibliography

The Broadmoor History, Colorado Springs.

Broadmoor Bonanza, Winter-Spring 1968, The Broadmoor Hotel publicity department.

Grand Trianon Art Museum

Ellis, Amanda M. *The Colorado Springs Story* Dentan Printing Co., Colorado Springs, 1954.

El Paso Club, 1968 Club Room, Colorado Springs.

The Newcomen Society of North America Colorado Springs, May 23, 1969.

Feitz, Leland. *Cripple Creek* The Dentan-Berkeland Printing Co., Colorado Springs, 1967.

Geiger, Helen M. *The Broadmoor Story* Smith Brooks, Colorado Springs, 1968.

The Zoo on the Mountain. Cheyenne Mountain Museum and Zoological Society, Colorado Springs, 1968.

Mazzulla, Fred & Jo. *The First 100 Years*, 1956.